Secrets and Mysteries of the Lost Ark

A Bible Adventure

James R. Hoffer

TEACH Services, Inc.
P U B L I S H I N G
www.TEACHServices.com • (800) 367-1844

Copyright © 2015 James R. Hoffer
Copyright © 2015 TEACH Services, Inc.
ISBN-13: 978-1-4796-0405-0 (Paperback)
ISBN-13: 978-1-4796-0406-7 (ePub)
ISBN-13: 978-1-4796-0407-4 (Mobi)
Library of Congress Control Number: 2014950814

Published by

TEACH Services, Inc.
P U B L I S H I N G
www.TEACHServices.com ● (800) 367-1844

Dedication

I lovingly dedicate this book to my dear wife, Vera—my faithful companion for more than fifty-three years. Survivor of the refugee camps of war-torn Europe, and more recently of the ravages of cancer, she remains a source of strength and inspiration to us all.

Acknowledgements

I am deeply indebted to my former teacher, mentor, and work supervisor during my college days, Dr. Leslie Hardinge. It was he who first inspired me in regard to what we call the "sanctuary message," during those very formative years of my educational experience at Washington Missionary College, later Columbia Union College, and now Washington Adventist University. He chose me at that tender age to be his research assistant and page composer as he prepared the very first edition of *Shadows of His Sacrifice*, which he continued to amplify throughout his life, and which now is considered to be one of the classic works on the subject. To this day, I treasure my well-worn personal copy, which dates back to the mimeograph era, as well as others of his books.

I also want to acknowledge Dr. Edward Heppenstall, one of my teachers at Andrews University Theological Seminary, who instilled in me a great love for the book of Hebrews.

And I would not want to forget Jesus Christ, my Lord and Savior, whose ministry in the heavenly sanctuary has been obscured for 2,000 years by layer upon layer of erroneous theology, and who sustains me every day by His power.

Table of Contents

Study Guide Answers

Introduction

Welcome to *Secrets and Mysteries of the Lost Ark: A Bible Adventure*. You are about to embark on a fascinating study. My hope is that as you dig into the Word of God your understanding of the sanctuary will deepen and grow as never before.

Many books, Bible studies, and seminars that deal with the sanctuary are very detailed and somewhat esoteric. Refreshingly, this series is more entry-level, becoming a platform for studying other important and often-neglected Bible truths and leading you into a closer walk with your Savior.

The sanctuary was and is both pageant and prophecy. In the daily and yearly ministrations of the Old Testament priests, the major events of God's plan of salvation were graphically portrayed. The books of Daniel, Hebrews, and Revelation reveal how each facet of the sanctuary relates to future events.

The sanctuary teaches us about God's character of love, justice, and holiness; His plan to save us and restore His lost planet to wholeness; the true cost of sin; and numerous other important concepts.

One Bible commentator wrote: "We are living in the last days, when error of a most deceptive character is accepted and believed, while truth is discarded.... *[God] calls upon us to work diligently in gathering up the jewels of truth, and placing them in the framework of the gospel.* In all their divine beauty they are to shine forth in the moral darkness of the world" (Ellen G. White, *Gospel Workers*, p. 289, emphasis mine).

The study of the Old Testament sanctuary has been largely neglected. It is my belief that the sanctuary message *is* the gospel, and provides a perfect framework for divine truth.

Above all, please pray for God's guidance through His Holy Spirit as you go through this series, for the study of the Bible is much more than an academic exercise—it is truly a life-changing experience. Are you ready to begin?

James R. Hoffer

Please note: These lessons are suitable for individual study, Bible classes, small groups, and public seminars. The book is divided into two sections with the study guide lessons in the first half and the study guide answers in the second half.

If you want to use this book for a class, students need their own book; it is not reproducible. For your convenience, PowerPoint slides are available upon request by visiting http://1ref.us/7e.

Any version of the Bible is quite acceptable for this seminar, although in these printed lessons the New King James Version is used in most cases.

Study Guide Lessons

Lesson 1

The Search for
the Lost Ark

The search for the ark of the covenant has long been a fascination of many people, and, of course, it was even enshrined in the movie *Raiders of the Lost Ark*. How it got "lost" in the first place is the subject of this first lesson.

1. What *three* arks are described in the Bible? (Gen. 6:11–17; Exod. 2:3; Exod. 25:10)

    a.

    b.

    c.

2. The ark we will be studying today is the third one, often called the "ark of the covenant." Where was this ark located? (Exod. 25:8; Heb. 9:3, 4)

    _____

    _____

    _____

> The ark was part of the furnishings of the sanctuary, or tabernacle, the portable structure that became the center of worship for the Israelites when they left Egypt and journeyed to the Promised Land after some 400 years of slavery.

3. What was the ark like? (Exod. 25:10–15)

_____

_____

4. What was placed on top of the ark? (Exod. 25:17–21; Heb. 9:5)

_____

_____

5. What was inside the ark? (Heb. 9:4; Deut. 10:2; see also 1 Kings 8:9)

   a.

   b.

   c.

_____

6. What was the purpose of the ark? (Exod. 25:22; Num. 7:89; Judges 20:27)

_____

_____

7. When is the ark mentioned in the Old Testament, and what role did it play in Jewish history?

    a.   Num. 10:33–35 _____

    b.   Josh. 3:3–17; 4:5–10 _____

    c.   Josh. 6:1–5 _____

    d.   1 Sam. 4–7 _____

    e.   2 Sam. 6:1–7 _____

    f.   1 Kings 8:1–11 _____

8. Who destroyed Solomon's temple, and what may have happened to the ark? (2 Chron. 36:15–21; Ezra 5:13–15; 6:1–5, 14, 15)

_____

_____

One commentator penned these words: "Among the righteous still in Jerusalem, to whom had been made plain the divine purpose, were some who determined to place beyond the reach of ruthless hands the sacred ark containing the tables of stone on which had been traced the precepts of the Decalogue. This they did. With mourning and sadness they secreted the ark in a cave, where it was to be hidden from the people of Israel and Judah because of their sins, and was to be no more restored to them. That sacred ark is yet hidden. It has never been disturbed since it was secreted" (Ellen G. White, *Prophets and Kings,* p. 453).

There is also a passage regarding this in the Apocrypha, in 2 Maccabees 2:4–8, claiming that Jeremiah hid the ark, the altar of incense, and even the tabernacle in a cave in Mount Nebo. This seems unlikely, as Nebo and the adjacent town of Madaba are in present-day Jordan, across the Jordan River and miles from Jerusalem. Plus, there was no tabernacle at that time, having been replaced many years previously by Solomon's temple.

9. A fourth ark appears in the Bible in the most surprising of places. Where is *that* ark? (Rev. 11:19)

The heavenly ark will be the subject of a future lesson. The earthly ark is probably hidden in a cave somewhere in Israel. It is interesting to note that the temple site in Jerusalem is now occupied by the Dome of the Rock, an Islamic holy place (pictured).

10. Where did King David delight to be? (Ps. 27:4; 69:9; 84:10; 122:1)

11. Which ark should I focus on now? (Heb. 8:1, 2; 9:11, 12)

Lesson 2

Jesus in the Sanctuary

No study of the ark would be complete without understanding the sanctuary, also referred to as the tabernacle or temple. "Sanctuary" means "holy place." It was not a church or place of assembly, but rather a gigantic visual aid meant to teach the people the basic principles of salvation and God's plan to restore all things.

1. Why is it important to understand the message of the sanctuary? (Ps. 73:1–17)

   _____

   _____

2. What was Jesus' first encounter with the temple? (Luke 2:21–40)

   _____

   _____

3. When did He next go to the temple? (Luke 2:41–52)

   _____

   _____

   _____

4. What must He have thought when He observed the animal sacrifices? (John 1:29; Rev. 5:6–14)

_____

_____

> "For the first time the child Jesus looked upon the temple. He saw the white-robed priests performing their solemn ministry. He beheld the bleeding victim upon the altar of sacrifice. With the worshipers He bowed in prayer, while the cloud of incense ascended before God. He witnessed the impressive rites of the paschal service. Day by day He saw their meaning more clearly. Every act seemed to be bound up with His own life. New impulses were awakening within Him. Silent and absorbed, He seemed to be studying out a great problem. The mystery of His mission was opening to the Saviour" (Ellen G. White, *The Desire of Ages*, p. 78).

5. When was the sacrificial system introduced and for what purpose? (Gen. 3:7, 21; 4:3–5; 22:1–14; Exod. 12:3–14)

_____

_____

6. Jesus often taught in the temple in Jerusalem during His ministry. On one particular occasion He used the sanctuary services to explain something about Himself. What truth did He share with the people? (John 7:37–39; Isa. 55:1)

_____

_____

_____

One Bible commentary gives us the following insight: "The flowing of the water from the rock in the desert was celebrated by the Israelites, after their establishment in Canaan, with demonstrations of great rejoicing. In the time of Christ this celebration had become a most impressive ceremony. It took place on the occasion of the Feast of Tabernacles, when the people from all the land were assembled at Jerusalem. On each of the seven days of the feast the priests went out with music and the choir of Levites to draw water in a golden vessel from the spring of Siloam. They were followed by multitudes of the worshipers, as many as could get near the stream drinking of it, while the jubilant strains arose, 'With joy shall ye draw water out of the wells of salvation.' Isaiah 12:3. Then the water drawn by the priests was borne to the temple amid the sounding of trumpets and the solemn chant, 'Our feet shall stand within thy gates, O Jerusalem.' Psalm 122:2. The water was poured out upon the altar of burnt offering, while songs of praise rang out, the multitudes joining in triumphant chorus with musical instruments and deep-toned trumpets.

"The Saviour made use of this symbolic service to direct the minds of the people to the blessings that He had come to bring them. 'In the last day, that great day of the feast,' His voice was heard in tones that rang through the temple courts, 'If any man thirst, let him come unto Me, and drink. He that believeth on Me, as the Scripture hath said, out of his belly shall flow rivers of living water.' 'This,' said John, 'spake He of the Spirit, which they that believe on Him should receive.' John 7:37–39. The refreshing water, welling up in a parched and barren land, causing the desert place to blossom, and flowing out to give life to the perishing, is an emblem of the divine grace which Christ alone can bestow, and which is as the living water, purifying, refreshing, and invigorating the soul. He in whom Christ is abiding has within him a never-failing fountain of grace and strength. Jesus cheers the life and brightens the path of all who truly seek Him. His love, received into the heart, will spring up in good works unto eternal life. And not only does it bless the soul in which it springs, but the living stream will flow out in words and deeds of righteousness, to refresh the thirsting around him.

"The same figure Christ had employed in His conversation with the woman of Samaria at Jacob's well: 'Whosoever drinketh of the water that I shall give him shall never thirst; but the water that I shall give him shall be in him a well of water springing up into everlasting life.' John 4:14. Christ combines the two types. He is the rock, He is the living water" (Ellen G. White, *Patriarchs and Prophets*, p. 412).

7. How does the sanctuary message reveal God's true character? (Isa. 14:12–14; Ezek. 28:12–19; Rev. 12:7–9)

_____

_____

8. What event in Christ's ministry especially portrayed His respect for the sanctuary? (Matt. 21:12, 13; John 2:13–16)

_____

_____

9. What happened at Christ's death that graphically showed how the earthly sanctuary services had met their fulfillment and would now completely lose their validity? (Matt. 27:45–51)

_____

_____

10. What is Christ's relationship with the heavenly sanctuary? (Heb. 7:28–8:6)

_____

_____

11. The sanctuary message holds the key to understanding the book of Revelation. What do the following passages teach about the heavenly sanctuary?

a. Rev. 1:10–20 _____

_____

b. Rev. 4:1–6_____

_____

c. Rev. 11:18, 19_____

_____

d. Rev. 15:1–6_____

_____

e. Rev. 21:22_____

_____

Lesson 3

Jesus Predicts the Destruction of the Temple

In our last lesson we saw how the sanctuary portrays the most basic of Christian doctrines—salvation through the atoning sacrifice of Christ—but that atonement process would not be complete without His second coming, which we will study about in this lesson.

1. The disciples were very proud of the temple. Its gleaming marble façade and beautiful furnishings topped the highest point in Jerusalem. One day when they were giving Jesus a tour of the "buildings of the temple," Jesus made a stunning prediction (Matt. 24:1, 2). A short while later, seated on a nearby hilltop, they confronted Jesus with what question? (Matt. 24:3)

    _____

    _____

2. Had the temple ever been destroyed before? Trace this brief history of the Jewish temple:

    a. 2 Sam. 7:1–13 _____

    b. 1 Kings 7:51–8:5 _____

c. 2 Chron. 36:15–21 _____

d. Ezra 3:10–13_____

3. We saw Jesus' great respect for the temple in our previous lesson, yet because the Jews as a whole rejected their Messiah, the temple was doomed again. Matthew 23 contains a series of "woes" against the scribes and Pharisees. What does Jesus say about Jerusalem in verses 37–39?

4. What were the two parts to the disciples' question in Matthew 24:3? And what was Jesus' response in the subsequent verses?

One account of the terrible destruction that occurred in AD 70 under the Roman general Titus reads as follows: "The blind obstinacy of the Jewish leaders, and the detestable crimes perpetrated within the besieged city, excited the horror and indignation of the Romans, and Titus at last decided to take the temple by storm. He determined, however, that if possible it should be saved from destruction. But his commands were disregarded. After he had retired to his tent at night, the Jews, sallying from the temple, attacked the soldiers without. In the struggle, a firebrand was flung by a soldier through an opening in the porch, and immediately the cedar-lined chambers about the holy house were in a blaze. Titus rushed to the place, followed by his generals and legionaries, and commanded the soldiers to quench the flames. His words were unheeded. In their fury the soldiers hurled blazing brands into the chambers adjoining the temple, and then with their swords they slaughtered in great numbers those who had found shelter there. Blood flowed down the temple steps like water. Thousands upon thousands of Jews perished. Above the sound of battle, voices were heard shouting: 'Ichabod!'—the glory is departed" (Ellen G. White, *The Great Controversy*, p. 33).

5. As you read Matthew 24, how many of the signs apply to either the destruction of Jerusalem or Christ's second coming, or both events?

    _____

    _____

6. What solemn warning did Jesus give us toward the end of His discourse in Matthew 24? (verse 44)

    _____

    _____

7. Several parables about "being ready" are found in Matthew 22 and 25. What lessons do they bring forth?

    a. The wedding feast (Matt. 22:1–14) _____

        _____

    b. The wise and foolish virgins (Matt. 25:1–13) _____

        _____

    c. The talents (Matt. 25:14–30) _____

        _____

   d.   The judgment (Matt. 25:31–46) _____

_____

> Note that according to several of Jesus' parables, the separation of the wicked and the righteous occurs only at the end of the world, and not at death (Matt. 13:24–30, 38–43; Matt. 13:47–50; Matt. 25:31–33).

8. How does the Bible describe Christ's second coming? (1 Thess. 4:13–18; 1 Cor. 15:51–54)

_____

_____

9. What does "as a thief in the night" mean? (1 Thess. 5:2; 2 Peter 3:10)

_____

10. God has promised us a new earth where we will be free at last from Satan and sin. What characteristics distinguish God's kingdom, which we will enjoy for eternity? (Rev. 21:4)

_____

_____

Lesson 4

The Covenant
of the Ark

There is a great deal of misunderstanding in the Christian world in regard to God's covenants with His people. This lesson will explore the Bible for important insight into the new covenant.

1. The ark in the sanctuary/tabernacle/temple was called "the ark of the covenant." This term is found forty-six times in the New King James Version Bible according to BibleGateway.com. Whose ark was it? (Num. 10:33; Josh. 3:11)

   _____

   _____

> Notice that when "Lord" is spelled with three small capital letters at the end (LORD), it is in place of "Jehovah" or "Jahweh" in the original Hebrew.

2. In general terms, what is a covenant? (Gen. 9:12–17)

   _____

   _____

3. What do we call God's covenant with humanity? (Heb. 13:20)

    _____

    _____

4. Why was the ark called "the ark of the covenant"? (Exod. 34:28)

    _____

    _____

5. There are many covenants in the Bible, but in this study we will focus on those covenants that have a bearing on our salvation. What can we learn from the following covenants?

    a. The "old covenant" between God and man (Gen. 2:16, 17)

        _____

    b. The "new covenant" after they sinned (Gen. 3:15)

        _____

    c. A trial run of the old covenant (Exod. 19:4–8; 24:3–7)

        _____

    d. The new covenant, enshrined in the ark (Exod. 25:8–22)

        _____

6. The two eternal principles of God's character and kingdom are perfect justice (based on the law) and perfect mercy. What are some major events of Bible history that trace these coexisting principles?

    a. Gen. 3:7, 21 _____

    b. Gen. 4:3–5 _____

    c.   Gen. 22:7–14 _____

    d.   Exod. 29:38, 39; Lev. 1:1–5 _____

    _____

    e.   Matt. 27:46–51 _____

7. What beautiful covenant term is used in the Bible to describe one's Christian relationship with the Savior?

    a.   Isa. 54:5_____

    b.   Rev. 21:9, 10_____

    c.   Eph. 5:22–32 _____

8. Were people in the Old Testament saved any differently than in the New Testament? (Isa. 55:6, 7; Ps. 51)

    _____

    _____

    _____

9. What are the important distinctions between the Ten Commandment law and the ceremonial law?

    a.   The Ten Commandments (Exod. 25:16, 21; 31:18; 40:20; Deut. 9:10)

    _____

    _____

    b.   The ceremonial law (Deut. 31:26)

    _____

    _____

10. Is the ceremonial law still applicable? (Heb. 9:9–12; Col. 2:14; Eph. 2:15; Heb. 10:1)

_____

_____

_____

_____

11. Is the moral law, the Ten Commandments, still applicable? (Ps. 19:7; Isa. 42:21; Matt. 5:18; Rom. 7:12; 3:31)

_____

_____

_____

_____

_____

12. What principles of the new covenant are important for us today?

    a.   Jer. 31:31–34; Ezek. 36:26, 27_____

    b.   Luke 22:20 _____

    c.   Heb. 8:1–6; Rev. 11:15–19 _____

13. What must I do to begin my journey with Christ and enter into a covenant relationship with Him? (Acts 16:31; Rom. 10:9; Col. 2:12; Gal. 3:27)

_____

_____

_____

Lesson 5

The Ark's Environment

The ark of the covenant was only one feature of the sanctuary. This lesson focuses on the other articles of furniture and their significance. God, who designed the sanctuary in the first place, gave each item deep meaning. The sanctuary, after all, was not a church or place of assembly as we think of today, but as was mentioned in lesson 2, the sanctuary was a divinely appointed visual aid, whose purpose was to portray various facets of His character of love and His plan to save fallen humanity.

1. Where did the design for the first sanctuary, or tabernacle, come from? (Exod. 25:1–9; 26:30)

   _____

   _____

   _____

   _____

2. Do you notice anything unique in Paul's overview of the tabernacle in Hebrews 9:1–10? (see also Exod. 31:1–11)

   _____

   _____

   _____

3. God is a God of detail. There was not a single element of the
    sanctuary left to the workers' imaginations. What are some of the
    features you notice in each of the areas?

    a. The courtyard (Exod. 27:9–19)

    _____

    _____

    _____

    b. The tabernacle itself (Exod. 26)

    _____

    _____

    _____

    c. The veil (Exod. 26:31–35; 30:6)

    _____

    _____

    _____

    d. The altar of burnt offering (Exod. 27:1–8)

    _____

    _____

    _____

    e. The laver (Exod. 30:17–21)

    _____

    _____

    _____

    f.   The table of showbread (Exod. 25:23–30)

_____

_____

    g.   The gold lampstand (Exod. 25:31–40)

_____

_____

    h.   The altar of incense (Exod. 30:1–10)

_____

_____

    i.   The ark of the covenant (Exod. 25:10–22)

_____

_____

    j.   The priestly garments (Exod. 28, especially verses 29, 30)

_____

_____

4. Let's now "enter" the sanctuary. How did the following things point forward to Jesus?

    a.   The altar of burnt offering (John 1:29; Heb. 7:25–27; 9:12)

_____

    b.   The gold lampstand (John 8:12)

_____

_____

    c.   The table of showbread (John 6:41–51)

    d.   The priest (Heb. 8:1, 2; 9:11, 12, 24)

5. Two major types of sacrifices were offered at the sanctuary. What were they?

    a.   Exod. 29:38–46

    b.   Lev. 4:1–6

6. Six special holy convocations or "feasts" were observed throughout the calendar year, three in the spring and three in the fall. What did they signify?

    a.   The Passover and Unleavened Bread (Lev. 23:4–8; 1 Cor. 5:7)

    b.   The Feast of Firstfruits (Harvest) (Lev. 23:9–14; Matt. 27:50–53)

    c.   The Feast of Weeks/Pentecost (Lev. 23:15–22; Acts 2:1–4)

    d.   The Feast of Trumpets (Lev. 23:23–25)

   e. The Day of Atonement (Lev. 23:26–32; 16:29, 30)

   _____

   f. The Feast of Tabernacles (Lev. 23:33–44)

   _____

7. Notice that the weekly Sabbath is mentioned separately in
    Leviticus 23:3. Why do you think the Sabbath is highlighted on
    its own?

    _____

    _____

8. As we study the sanctuary, it becomes ever clearer that God
    is trying to teach us two great salvation principles. What two
    principles are they?

    a. _____

    b. _____

9. How is this portrayed in the overall design of the sanctuary?

    a. The Holy Place and the "daily" service (Heb. 9:6)

    _____

    b. The Most Holy Place and the "yearly" service (Heb. 9:7)

    _____

10. What important lesson can be learned from the sanctuary,
    especially from the golden lampstand? (Ps. 119:105)

    _____

    _____

The Earthly Sanctuary

"The sanctuary was and is both *pageant* and *prophecy*."

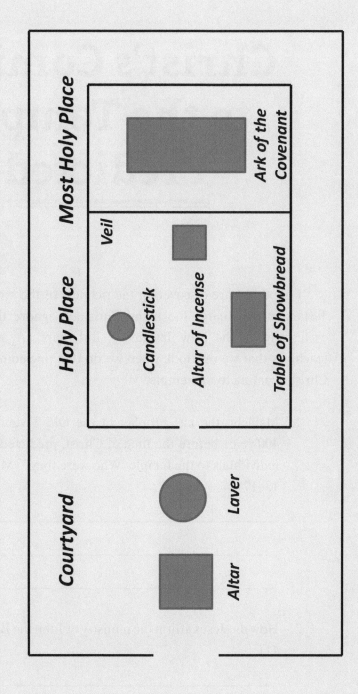

Christ's Coming to the Temple Predicted

I hope you are discovering the richness of the symbolism in the Old Testament sanctuary. Too many Christians ignore this part and focus exclusively on the New Testament. But there are so many wonderful teachings that we overlook when we do that, including the prediction of Christ's coming to the temple.

1. Malachi, the last prophet in the Old Testament, writing about 400 years before the time of Christ, predicted the coming of two individuals to the temple. Who were they? (Mal. 3:1; Matt. 3:1–3, 13–17)

   _____

   _____

   _____

2. How did Jesus affirm the ministry of John the Baptist? (Matt. 11:7–11)

   _____

   _____

3. What prophecy of Malachi did Jesus link to John the Baptist? (Mal. 4:5, 6; John 1:19–23; Matt. 11:12–14)

_____

_____

4. Did Jesus come to earth at a particular time in history? (Gal. 4:4, 5; Mark 1:14, 15)

_____

_____

5. The Bible contains a few prophecies that are linked to a particular time, and we are now going to look at one of them. What precedent do we have for interpreting the time factor a certain way? (Ezek. 4:1–6)

_____

_____

_____

6. This, then, is the "day for a year" principle, which can safely be applied to many time prophecies. Daniel was one of those exiles who distinguished himself in that setting and was elevated to leadership in the Babylonian government, and later in the successor government of Persia. What is the sequence of events outlined in Daniel 9?

    a. Dan. 9:1, 2; Jer. 25:11, 12

_____

_____

_____

   b.   Dan. 9:3–19

_____

_____

   c.   Dan. 9:20–23

_____

_____

_____

7. As we unpack the significance of Gabriel's words, we see a time prophecy that accurately predicted Christ's first coming. If our time prophecy ruler holds true, that a prophetic "day" equals a literal year, how many years would the seventy-weeks prophecy signify? And what do the phrases "are determined" and "for your people" mean? (Dan. 9:24)

_____

_____

_____

8. What were they supposed to accomplish during the seventy-weeks period? Did they succeed? (Dan 9:24; Matt. 23:37–39)

_____

_____

_____

9. What event signaled the beginning of the prophecy? (Dan. 9:25)

_____

_____

10. Do we have a copy of this decree that was the catalyst for the prophecy? (Ezra 7:11–26)

_____

_____

11. When was the Messiah, Jesus, supposed to come to His temple? (Dan. 9:26)

_____

12. What would happen to the temple some years after Christ's death? (Matt. 24:1, 2, 15–20)

_____

13. How would Christ "confirm a covenant for one week" with the Jews? (Matt. 10:5, 6; Acts 13:42–46)

_____

_____

_____

14. Was God's covenant with Israel conditional or unconditional? (Deut. 28:1, 2, 15, 16)

_____

15. Exactly when did Christ die on Calvary? (Dan. 9:27)

_____

16. What event showed that the temple sacrifices were abolished, at least in God's eyes? (Matt. 27:51)

_____

17. Who are God's people today? (Gal. 6:15, 16; 3:27–29; Rom. 9:6–8; 11:5, 13–17, 26)

_____

_____

"In the middle of the week He shall bring an end to sacrifice and offering." – Dan. 9:27

70 "weeks" = 490 years

2,300 "days" = 2,300 years

457 BC

27-31-34 AD

Courtyard

Altar

Laver

Holy Place

Most Holy Place

Candlestick

Altar of Incense

Table of Showbread

Veil

Ark of the Covenant

Lesson 7

The Cleansing of the Temple

Isn't it amazing to discover that the sanctuary not only portrayed the *events* in Christ's life and ministry but the very *timing* of those events? This is exciting news, and something that many Christians miss entirely. Today we continue our journey into the study of this amazing timeline prophesied in Daniel 8 and 9.

1. How do we know that the prophecies of Daniel 8 and 9 are linked? (Dan. 8:27; 9:1–3, 20–23)

     _____

     _____

2. What strange figures appear in his vision in chapter 8, and what do they represent? (Dan. 8:1–9)

     _____

     _____

3. How did the little horn desecrate the sanctuary? (Dan. 8:10–12)

     _____

     _____

4. How long would it be until the sanctuary truth was restored? (Dan. 8:13, 14)

_____

_____

5. When did that period begin? (Dan. 9:25)

_____

_____

6. The term "cleansing of the sanctuary" was well understood by the Jews to refer to the Day of Atonement, which in turn signified the judgment. Once a year this pageant was re-enacted in a ceremony that focused on the Most Holy Place. What did this ceremony signify? (Lev. 23:26–32; 16:29, 30)

_____

_____

7. The sanctuary ceremonies are divided into two basic parts: the "daily" and the "yearly" services. What was represented by the daily services? (Mark 15:33–39)

_____

_____

8. So if the daily service is prophetic, what then does the yearly service foretell? (Rev. 20:11–15)

_____

_____

9. Notice Daniel's prophecy of the judgment. What takes place before Christ returns to the earth? (Dan. 7:9, 10)

10. What solemn sanctuary ceremony portrays God's saving grace? (Lev. 16:7–10)

    _____

    a. Whom does the Lord's goat represent? _____

    b. Whom does the scapegoat (Azazel) represent? _____

    c. When does the Lord's goat die? (Lev. 16:8, 9; John 19:28–
        30) _____

    d. When does the scapegoat die? (Lev. 16:10; Rev. 20:7–10)

    _____

    _____

    _____

    _____

11. Some believe that both goats represent Christ. If both goats had to be perfect, how can we say that Azazel represents Satan? (Ezek. 28:12–15)

    _____

12. In what sense is "atonement" used in Leviticus 16:15–22?

    _____

    _____

    _____

13. What happened in 1844 that makes it a significant time in Bible
   prophecy? (Rev. 10:8–11)

_____

_____

_____

_____

Following the symbolism of the sanctuary to its logical
conclusion, we believe that part of the judgment began in 1844. We
call it the "investigative judgment" because Christ is preparing us for
His coming. There is a definite sense in which we, too, should "afflict
our souls" as the Israelites did on the Day of Atonement by taking life
seriously and living for Jesus.

14. Will we ever have to deal with sin again? (Nahum 1:9)

_____

_____

"For two thousand three hundred days; then the sanctuary shall be cleansed." – Dan. 8:14

70 "weeks" = 490 years

1810 years

2,300 "days" = 2,300 years

457 BC

27-31-34 AD

1844 AD

Courtyard

Altar

Laver

Holy Place

Candlestick

Altar of Incense

Table of Showbread

Veil

Most Holy Place

Ark of the Covenant

The Contents of the Ark

In lesson 1 we briefly referred to the contents of the ark of the covenant, but today we are going to look at their deeper significance. The ark was the holiest item in the sanctuary because it represented the very presence of God.

1. How was the ark constructed?

    a. What was its size? (Exod. 25:10)

    _____

    b. What was it made out of? (verses 10, 11)

    _____

    c. How was it to be transported? (verses 12–15)

    _____

    d. What went inside the ark? (verse 16)

    _____

    e. What was placed on top of the ark? (verses 17–21)

    _____

f.   What activity was to take place in front of the ark? (verse 22)

_____

2. What other items would later be added to the ark? (Heb. 9:4; Exod. 16:33, 34; Num. 17:1–10)

_____

3. What do the following items represent in relation to God and His character?

a.   The Ten Commandments _____

b.   The manna _____

c.   Aaron's rod _____

d.   The mercy seat_____

e.   The cherubim_____

4. Why is it important for us to have a true picture of God? (Isa. 14:12–15)

_____

_____

_____

We have all heard statements like, "If there is a God, He would not permit …" Satan takes great delight in these assaults on God's character. The truth is that God is the healer and deliverer, and Satan the destroyer and warmonger.

5. What insight does Jesus' statement to the disciples give us about the blind man and his suffering? (John 9:1–5)

_____

_____

6. What did the apostle Paul say about his struggle with infirmity and the role Satan played? (2 Cor. 12:7–10)

_____

_____

7. What does the story of Job teach us about Satan's involvement on this earth? (Job 1:6–12)

_____

If God were to suddenly wipe out all of earth's misery, poverty, disease, and death, we would not look forward to heaven. And if God healed only Christians, then many would become a Christian for the wrong reason.

8. Returning to the ark, what are the two basic salvation principles that it teaches us?

a. The Ten Commandments (Rev. 14:12; 22:14; Matt. 5:17, 18; Rom. 3:20, 31; 7:12)

_____

_____

b. The mercy seat (Rom. 3:23, 24; 5:1; James 2:10–12; 1 John 1:9)

_____

_____

9. How did God present Himself to Moses? What character traits did God use to describe Himself? (Exod. 34:5, 6; Ps. 85:10)

_____

_____

10. What other important characteristic of God is highlighted in the Bible? (Ps. 115:1–8)

_____

11. Is there anything in the ark of the covenant that alludes to God as our Creator? (Exod. 20:8–11)

_____

_____

_____

12. What do the following texts teach us about the Sabbath day?

    a. Gen. 2:1–3 _____

    _____

    b. Mark 2:27, 28 _____

    _____

    c. Exod. 16:23–29 _____

    _____

    d. Neh. 13:15–22 _____

    _____

    e. Acts 13:42–44; 16:13 _____

    _____

f.   Heb. 4:8, 9 _____

_____

g.   Isa. 66:22, 23_____

_____

13. If keeping the law doesn't actually save us, what good is the law, and do we need to follow it? (James 1:22–25; Rom. 3:20)

_____

_____

"The precious record of the law was placed in the ark of the testament and is still there, safely hidden from the human family. But in God's appointed time He will bring forth these tables of stone to be a testimony to all the world against the disregard of His commandments and against the idolatrous worship of a counterfeit Sabbath" (Ellen G. White, *Manuscript Releases*, vol. 8, p. 100).

Lesson 9

Parables of the Kingdom

The people of Jesus' day, including His own disciples, had some very twisted notions in regard to the kingdom of God. They were looking for a Messiah who would overthrow the oppressive Romans and restore the nation to earthly greatness. In this lesson we will explore the parables that Jesus told as He patiently explained the true nature of His kingdom and the final events that would usher it in.

1. What do the following parables of Jesus teach us about the *timing* of the day of judgment?

    a. The wheat and tares (Matt. 13:24–30, 36–43)

    b. The dragnet (Matt. 13:47–50)

    c. The final judgment (Matt. 25:31–34, 41)

    _____

    _____

    _____

    _____

    _____

2. What can we learn from the following supporting scriptures?

   a. Dan. 7:9, 10 _____

   b. Acts 24:15 _____

   c. Mark 13:24–27 _____

   d. John 5:28, 29 _____

   e. Acts 2:29–35 _____

   f. 1 Cor. 15:51–54; 1 Thess. 4:13–17 _____

   _____

3. In lesson 7 we learned that a facet of the judgment began in the year 1844. What does this entail? (Dan. 7:9, 10)

   _____

   _____

   _____

   _____

4. When does the verdict phase occur? (2 Thess. 2:8; Rev. 6:15–17)

   _____

5. Is that it for the wicked? What is the sequence of events outlined in Revelation 19 and 20?

   a. Rev. 19:11–16 _____

   b. Rev. 19:17–21 _____

   c. Rev. 20:1–3 _____

    d.   Rev. 20:4–6; 1 Cor. 6:2, 3 _____

    e.   Rev. 20:7–14_____

6. The whole book of Revelation is bathed in sanctuary language. What do you notice in the following passages?

    a.   Rev. 1:9–20_____

    b.   Rev. 4 _____

    c.   Rev. 8:1–6_____

    d.   Rev. 11:1–3_____

    e.   Rev. 15:5–8_____

    _____

    _____

7. What event is described in Revelation 14:14–16?

    _____

8. Does God seek to catch us off guard with His coming, or does He give us forewarning? (Matt. 24:25; Jonah 3:1–4)

    _____

9. How does God warn the world just prior to Christ's coming? (Rev. 14:6–13)

    _____

    _____

    _____

10. We now examine the three angels' messages in some detail. What are the components of the first angel's message? (Rev. 14:6, 7)

    a. Flying in the midst of heaven _____

    b. The everlasting gospel _____

    c. To every nation _____

    d. Fear God, give Him glory _____

    e. The hour of judgment _____

    f. Worship the Creator _____

11. What do we learn about the second angel's message? (Rev. 14:8; see also Rev. 17 and 18, especially 18:1–4)

    _____

    _____

12. What does the third angel proclaim? (Rev. 14:9–11)

    _____

    _____

13. In direct contrast to the wicked in Babylon, how are the righteous described just before Christ's coming? (Rev. 14:12, 13)

    _____

    _____

Lesson 10

Holiness to the Lord

When the people of Israel were freed from hundreds of years of enslavement in the land of Egypt, to a great degree they had lost their faith and had to be completely re-educated in the things of the Lord and in basic life principles. Notable exceptions would include Moses' parents and a handful of faithful Israelites, for we know that God has always preserved His truth throughout history, even if it often went underground. Once the Israelites set up camp in the wilderness, it was no longer practical for each family to individually practice the sacrificial rituals at home, so the sanctuary system was introduced. This lesson focuses on the concept of holiness.

1. What visible sign of holiness was part of the priest's garment? (Exod. 28:36–38; 39:30, 31)

    _____

2. What does it mean to be "holy"? (1 Peter 1:16; Matt. 5:48)

    _____

    _____

3. How did God begin to reveal His plan of holiness to the people through Moses? (Exod. 3:1–5)

    _____

    _____

4. How did God set forth this ideal before the people as a whole? (Exod. 19:3–6; 20:8)

_____

_____

_____

5. What experience on the journey to Canaan underlined the urgency of the concept of holiness? (Lev. 10:1–10)

_____

_____

6. In what other way was holiness to be reflected in their lifestyle? (Lev. 11:44–47; Acts 10:9–16, 28)

_____

_____

_____

_____

7. God challenges us to achieve holiness in every area of our lives, such as:

   a. 1 Cor. 3:16 _____

   b. 1 Cor. 6:9–11; 18–20 _____

   c. Lev. 27:30; Mal. 3:8–10 _____

8. The concept of holiness is carried throughout the Bible. What can we learn about this concept in the Old and New Testaments? (Ezek. 22:26; 44:16–23; 1 Peter 2:9)

_____

_____

_____

_____

9. What medieval theology obliterated the "priesthood of the believer" and became an issue in the Protestant Reformation?

_____

_____

10. What happened to the priesthood when Christ died? (Matt. 27:51; Heb. 8:1–6)

_____

11. In what sense do we serve as "priests" today? (John 21:15–17; 1 Peter 5:3–5)

_____

12. What postmodern concept has blurred the distinction between the holy and the unholy?

_____

_____

_____

13. What perspective will help us dedicate our lives completely to God? (Heb. 11:13; 1 Peter 2:11)

_____

_____

14. Becoming "holy" is clearly a foreign concept to the world in general. How does the Lord counsel us to put life in perspective and put Him first so that by association with Him we can become holy?

    a.   1 John 2:15–17 _____

    b.   2 Peter 3:10–13_____

Let us all pray that the Lord will do His wonderful work in our lives, and thus prepare us for His heavenly kingdom! "Prayer is heaven's ordained means of success in the conflict with sin and the development of Christian character. The divine influences that come in answer to the prayer of faith will accomplish in the soul of the supplicant all for which he pleads. For the pardon of sin, for the Holy Spirit, for a Christlike temper, for wisdom and strength to do His work, for any gift He has promised, we may ask; and the promise is, 'Ye shall receive'" (Ellen G. White, *The Acts of the Apostles*, p. 564).

Lesson 11

Heavenly Mediation

Especially in today's world, man is considered independent and self-sufficient. "Freedom" for many is interpreted to mean that morally we answer to no one, that we are autonomous. Closely related to that is the idea of relativism—what I believe may differ from what you believe, and we are both right! "Truth" is OK for the mathematician, the physicist, the chemist, etc., but behavioral truth doesn't exist and is conditioned by our culture and upbringing. The sad results of these philosophies are all around us.

1. In the parable of the lost sheep, was the sheep "free"? (Luke 15:3–7)

    _____

    _____

2. What was Jesus' mission while on earth? (Luke 19:10)

    _____

    _____

3. Jesus' mediation began while on earth. For whom did He intercede? (John 17:6–21)

    _____

4. What is the only way to be truly free? (John 17:17; 14:6; 8:30–36)

    _____

5. What does the sanctuary teach us about Jesus, our Savior and Mediator?

    a. Heb. 9:12 _____

    b. Heb. 8:1, 2, 6 _____

    c. Heb. 9:28 _____

    _____

6. What qualifies Christ to be our Mediator? (Heb. 4:15, 16; 5:8, 9)

    _____

    _____

7. What do the following scriptures teach us regarding the mediation of Christ?

    a. 1 Tim. 2:5, 6 _____

    b. Heb. 8:6; 9:15 _____

    _____

    c. John 14:1–6 _____

    _____

> It is important to note that some theological systems point to other "mediators," such as priests, Mary, etc. These erroneous ideas arose during the great apostasy of Christianity after the time of the apostles.

8. If Jesus is mediating for us in the heavenly sanctuary, who is here on earth helping us? (John 16:7)

    _____

9. What is the Holy Spirit's work? (John 16:8–13)

    _____

10. What qualifies us to benefit from the Holy Spirit's work?
    (John 14:15–17; Heb. 10:14)

    _____

    _____

    _____

11. How can we find this truth? (John 18:36–38)

    _____

    _____

12. What is the Holy Spirit's role when we pray? (Rom. 8:26, 27)

    _____

13. How does the Holy Spirit empower us to serve others? (1 Cor. 12:1,
    7–11)

    _____

14. How do Christ and the Holy Spirit open the doors of heaven for
    us right now? (Eph. 3:12; Heb. 4:16)

    _____

15. All the truths we have studied today emanate from the sanctuary.
    How did the psalmists express their joy regarding God's house?
    (Ps. 77:13; 122:1)

    _____

16. What happened in the days of King Josiah when the Scriptures were rediscovered? (2 Kings 22:8–13)

_____

17. When Huldah the prophetess was consulted, what did she say, especially to the young king? (2 Kings 22:15–20)

_____

May we humble our hearts to receive the Word of God and surrender our lives to Jesus!

Lesson 12

The Ark of Safety

We begin our final lesson with this quote from *The Great Controversy*: "The subject of the sanctuary was the key which unlocked the mystery of the disappointment of 1844. *It opened to view a complete system of truth, connected and harmonious*, showing that God's hand had directed the great advent movement and revealing present duty as it brought to light the position and work of His people" (Ellen G. White, p. 423, emphasis mine).

We could discuss the quest for the earthly ark of the covenant but that would only satisfy a curiosity to solve the mystery of its location. In this final lesson, let's devote our time to studying the heavenly ark, which has been obscured by several layers of false theology through the centuries. Satan succeeded in grand measure in directing mankind's focus away from Christ and to a visible "kingdom" on earth to create a dependency on a church system rather than on the ministry of our heavenly high priest.

1. What earthly system prevailed during the Dark Ages, and what means did it use to draw attention to itself and away from Christ? (Dan. 8:9; Rev. 13:6)

    _____

    _____

2. What are the main characteristics that help us identify this power? (Dan. 8:9–12; Rev. 13:1–8)

    _____

    _____

3. When would this false system be unmasked? (Dan. 8:13, 14; Heb. 9:23)

"This prophetic period came to its close on October 22, 1844. The disappointment to those who expected to meet their Lord on that day was great. Hiram Edson, a careful Bible student in mid-New York State, describes what took place among the company of believers of which he was a part:

"'Our expectations were raised high, and thus we looked for our coming Lord until the clock tolled twelve at midnight. The day had then passed, and our disappointment had become a certainty. Our fondest hopes and expectations were blasted, and such a spirit of weeping came over us as I never experienced before. It seemed that the loss of all earthly friends could have been no comparison. We wept and wept, till the day dawn....

"'I mused in my heart, saying: "My advent experience has been the brightest of all my Christian experience.... Has the Bible proved a failure? Is there no God, no heaven, no golden city, no Paradise? Is all this but a cunningly devised fable? Is there no reality to our fondest hopes and expectations?"...

"'I began to feel there might be light and help for us in our distress. I said to some of the brethren: "Let us go to the barn." We entered the granary, shut the doors about us, and bowed before the Lord. We prayed earnestly, for we felt our necessity. We continued in earnest prayer until the witness of the Spirit was given that our prayers were accepted, and that light should be given—our disappointment explained, made clear and satisfactory.

"'After breakfast I said to one of my brethren, "Let us go and see and encourage some of our brethren." We started, and while passing through a large field, I was stopped about midway of the field. Heaven seemed open to my view, and I saw distinctly and clearly that instead of our High Priest coming out of the most holy place of the heavenly sanctuary to this earth on the tenth day of the seventh month, at the end of the 2300 days, He, for the first time, entered on that day into the second apartment of that sanctuary, and that He had a work to perform in the most holy place before coming to the earth; that He came to the marriage, or in other words, to the Ancient of Days, to receive a kingdom, dominion, and glory; and that we must wait for His return from the wedding. And my mind was directed to the tenth chapter of Revelation, where I could see the vision had spoken and did not lie'—Unpublished manuscript published in part in The Review and Herald, June 23, 1921" (Ellen G. White, *Christ in His Sanctuary*, p. 5).

4. Who is the Prince of the host? (Josh. 5:13–15; Dan. 9:25; 10:21; 12:1)

   _____

5. In what specific ways did the little horn's theology succeed in replacing Jesus' ministry?

   a. A wrong priesthood (Rev. 1:6; 1 Peter 2:9)

   _____

   _____

   _____

   b. A false mediatorial system (Heb. 8:1–6)

   _____

   _____

   c. A false religious system with its mystical trappings such as burning incense, statues and icons, an altar-centered and divided chancel, holy water, relics, and other such non-biblical things.

   _____

_____

_____

_____

_____

Hebrews 9:24 reveals that the earthly sanctuary and its furnishings were only "copies of the true." Therefore, the real "lost ark" was rediscovered in 1844, in a cornfield, by a dedicated layperson! This ark, the heavenly sanctuary, and the heavenly ministry of Jesus came to light and resulted in a new Christian movement known as the Seventh-day Adventist Church. What are the "secrets and mysteries" of this "lost ark"? They are only secrets and mysteries because most people never study the sanctuary, and so the ark has become lost.

Note: The Seventh-day Adventist Church holds many of its teachings in common with other denominations, but it is the *only* one that teaches the sanctuary message!

---

6. So in review, and according to what we have discovered through this series of lessons, what are some of the major Bible teachings given to us in the sanctuary message—the "jewels of truth" that should be placed "in the framework of the gospel" (Ellen G. White, *Gospel Workers*, p. 289)?

    a. Heb. 9:11, 12 _____

    b. Isa. 14:12–14_____

    c. 1 Thess. 4:16–18_____

    d. Dan. 8:14; Rev. 14:6, 7 _____

    e. John 14:15, 16; Rom. 6:23_____

"In the holiest I saw an ark; on the top and sides of it was purest gold. On each end of the ark was a lovely cherub, with its wings spread out over it. Their faces were turned toward each other, and they looked downward. Between the angels was a golden censer. Above the ark, where the angels stood, was an exceeding bright glory, that appeared like a throne where God dwelt. Jesus stood by the ark, and as the saints' prayers came up to Him, the incense in the censer would smoke, and He would offer up their prayers with the smoke of the incense to His Father. In the ark was the golden pot of manna, Aaron's rod that budded, and the tables of stone which folded together like a book. Jesus opened them, and I saw the ten commandments written on them with the finger of God. On one table were four, and on the other six. The four on the first table shone brighter than the other six. But the fourth, the Sabbath commandment, shone above them all; for the Sabbath was set apart to be kept in honor of God's holy name. The holy Sabbath looked glorious—a halo of glory was all around it. I saw that the Sabbath commandment was not nailed to the cross. If it was, the other nine commandments were; and we are at liberty to break them all, as well as to break the fourth. I saw that God had not changed the Sabbath, for He never changes" (Ellen G. White, *Early Writings*, pp. 32, 33).

7. Given that there has been so much distortion throughout the centuries, is "church" really a necessity in the believer's life? Is God somehow in the church? (Matt. 16:16–19; 1 Peter 2:6–10; Heb. 12:22, 23)

_____

_____

_____

_____

8. What indication do we have that tells us that Jesus loves the church? (Eph. 5:25–27; Rev. 1:12–20)

_____

9. How was the organization of the early church set up, which serves as our pattern today? (Acts 6:1–7; 14:23; 15:1–3)

_____

_____

10. How were members added to the church? (Acts 2:41–47)

_____

11. There were only eight people saved on Noah's ark. What does Peter say is the antitype that now saves us? (1 Peter 3:18–22)

_____

_____

Our early believers often used the term "ark of safety" to refer to the church. This, then, is the Bible's fifth ark! In Noah's day, the people who listened to him had a choice to either get on the boat or not. It is no different today. All four arks we identified in lesson one were and are "arks of safety." The following quote provides us insight into the ark of safety and our role in sharing this message with others.

"There is work to be done for our neighbors and for those with whom we associate. We have no liberty to cease our patient, prayerful labors for souls as long as any are out of the ark of safety. There is no release in this war. We are soldiers of Christ, and are under obligation to watch lest the enemy gain the advantage and secure to his service souls that we might win to Christ" (Ellen G. White, *Testimonies for the Church*, vol. 5, p. 279).

Study Guide
Answers

Lesson 1

The Search for the Lost Ark

The search for the ark of the covenant has long been a fascination of many people, and, of course, it was even enshrined in the movie *Raiders of the Lost Ark.* How it got "lost" in the first place is the subject of this first lesson.

1. What *three* arks are described in the Bible? (Gen. 6:11–17; Exod. 2:3; Exod. 25:10)

   a. Noah's ark

   b. Baby Moses' ark

   c. The ark of the covenant

2. The ark we will be studying today is the third one, often called the "ark of the covenant." Where was this ark located? (Exod. 25:8; Heb. 9:3, 4)
   In the Most Holy Place of the sanctuary.

> The ark was part of the furnishings of the sanctuary, or tabernacle, the portable structure that became the center of worship for the Israelites when they left Egypt and journeyed to the Promised Land after some 400 years of slavery.

3. What was the ark like? (Exod. 25:10–15)

    The ark was a golden chest. The New Living Translation of verse 10 calculates the size of this golden chest as "a sacred chest 45 inches long, 27 inches wide, and 27 inches high."

4. What was placed on top of the ark? (Exod. 25:17–21; Heb. 9:5)

    The mercy seat with two cherubim of gold, one on each end of the mercy seat. "Cherubim" are angels, in this case representing the angels that are closest to God on His heavenly throne.

5. What was inside the ark? (Heb. 9:4; Deut. 10:2; see also 1 Kings 8:9)

    a. Pot of manna

    b. Aaron's rod

    c. Ten Commandments; notice that the Ten Commandments are also called "the testimony" and "the tablets of the covenant."

6. What was the purpose of the ark? (Exod. 25:22; Num. 7:89; Judges 20:27)

    It represented God's throne and His presence among His people.

7. When is the ark mentioned in the Old Testament, and what role did it play in Jewish history?

   a. Num. 10:33–35 – The ark went before the people to guide them.

   b. Josh. 3:3–17; 4:5–10 – The ark was used in the crossing of the Jordan River.

   c. Josh. 6:1–5 – The ark was carried around Jericho.

   d. 1 Sam. 4–7 – The ark was captured and returned by the Philistines.

   e. 2 Sam. 6:1–7 – Uzzah touched the ark and died as a result of his disobedience.

   f. 1 Kings 8:1–11 – The ark was placed in Solomon's temple.

8. Who destroyed Solomon's temple, and what may have happened to the ark? (2 Chron. 36:15–21; Ezra 5:13–15; 6:1–5, 14, 15)

   The temple was plundered by the Babylonians when they captured Jerusalem. The ark disappeared at that time.

One commentator penned these words: "Among the righteous still in Jerusalem, to whom had been made plain the divine purpose, were some who determined to place beyond the reach of ruthless hands the sacred ark containing the tables of stone on which had been traced the precepts of the Decalogue. This they did. With mourning and sadness they secreted the ark in a cave, where it was to be hidden from the people of Israel and Judah because of their sins, and was to be no more restored to them. That sacred ark is yet hidden. It has never been disturbed since it was secreted" (Ellen G. White, *Prophets and Kings,* p. 453).

There is also a passage regarding this in the Apocrypha, in 2 Maccabees 2:4–8, claiming that Jeremiah hid the ark, the altar of incense, and even the tabernacle in a cave in Mount Nebo. This seems unlikely, as Nebo and the adjacent town of Madaba are in present-day Jordan, across the Jordan River and miles from Jerusalem. Plus, there was no tabernacle at that time, having been replaced many years previously by Solomon's temple.

9. A fourth ark appears in the Bible in the most surprising of places. Where is *that* ark? (Rev. 11:19)

   That ark is found in heaven!

The heavenly ark will be the subject of a future lesson. The earthly ark is probably hidden in a cave somewhere in Israel. It is interesting to note that the temple site in Jerusalem is now occupied by the Dome of the Rock, an Islamic holy place (pictured).

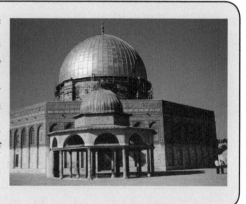

10. Where did King David delight to be? (Ps. 27:4; 69:9; 84:10; 122:1)

   King David delighted to be in the presence of the Lord in His house, which, at that time, was still the tabernacle.

11. Which ark should I focus on now? (Heb. 8:1, 2; 9:11, 12)

   The rest of our study will focus on the heavenly sanctuary and the ark where Jesus is ministering before He returns to this earth.

Lesson 2

Jesus in the Sanctuary

No study of the ark would be complete without understanding the sanctuary, also referred to as the tabernacle or temple. "Sanctuary" means "holy place." It was not a church or place of assembly, but rather a gigantic visual aid meant to teach the people the basic principles of salvation and God's plan to restore all things.

1. Why is it important to understand the message of the sanctuary? (Ps. 73:1–17)

    When correctly understood, the sanctuary answers the "big questions" about the existence of evil and the problem of human suffering.

2. What was Jesus' first encounter with the temple? (Luke 2:21–40)

    His dedication as a baby was His first visit to the temple.

3. When did He next go to the temple? (Luke 2:41–52)

    When He turned twelve, like all Jewish boys, He was allowed to participate in the Passover service. He traveled with Mary and Joseph to Jerusalem upon reaching manhood according to Jewish custom.

4. What must He have thought when He observed the animal sacrifices? (John 1:29; Rev. 5:6–14)

> The Holy Spirit impressed upon Him that He was the Lamb of God who was to save the people from their sins.

"For the first time the child Jesus looked upon the temple. He saw the white-robed priests performing their solemn ministry. He beheld the bleeding victim upon the altar of sacrifice. With the worshipers He bowed in prayer, while the cloud of incense ascended before God. He witnessed the impressive rites of the paschal service. Day by day He saw their meaning more clearly. Every act seemed to be bound up with His own life. New impulses were awakening within Him. Silent and absorbed, He seemed to be studying out a great problem. The mystery of His mission was opening to the Saviour" (Ellen G. White, *The Desire of Ages*, p. 78).

---

5. When was the sacrificial system introduced and for what purpose? (Gen. 3:7, 21; 4:3–5; 22:1–14; Exod. 12:3–14)

> God introduced the sacrificial system to Adam and Eve and their descendants after they left the Garden of Eden. After the Exodus, He enshrined it in the sanctuary services. The sacrifices were to symbolize that the penalty of sin is death (Rom. 6:23).

6. Jesus often taught in the temple in Jerusalem during His ministry. On one particular occasion, He used the sanctuary services to explain something about Himself. What truth did He share with the people? (John 7:37–39; Isa. 55:1)

> He told the people that He is the Water of Life, the only One who can satisfy (see also John 4:13, 14).

One Bible commentary gives us the following insight: "The flowing of the water from the rock in the desert was celebrated by the Israelites, after their establishment in Canaan, with demonstrations of great rejoicing. In the time of Christ this celebration had become a most impressive ceremony. It took place on the occasion of the Feast of Tabernacles, when the people from all the land were assembled at Jerusalem. On each of the seven days of the feast the priests went out with music and the choir of Levites to draw water in a golden vessel from the spring of Siloam. They were followed by multitudes of the worshipers, as many as could get near the stream drinking of it, while the jubilant strains arose, 'With joy shall ye draw water out of the wells of salvation.' Isaiah 12:3. Then the water drawn by the priests was borne to the temple amid the sounding of trumpets and the solemn chant, 'Our feet shall stand within thy gates, O Jerusalem.' Psalm 122:2. The water was poured out upon the altar of burnt offering, while songs of praise rang out, the multitudes joining in triumphant chorus with musical instruments and deep-toned trumpets.

"The Saviour made use of this symbolic service to direct the minds of the people to the blessings that He had come to bring them. 'In the last day, that great day of the feast,' His voice was heard in tones that rang through the temple courts, 'If any man thirst, let him come unto Me, and drink. He that believeth on Me, as the Scripture hath said, out of his belly shall flow rivers of living water.' 'This,' said John, 'spake He of the Spirit, which they that believe on Him should receive.' John 7:37–39. The refreshing water, welling up in a parched and barren land, causing the desert place to blossom, and flowing out to give life to the perishing, is an emblem of the divine grace which Christ alone can bestow, and which is as the living water, purifying, refreshing, and invigorating the soul. He in whom Christ is abiding has within him a never-failing fountain of grace and strength. Jesus cheers the life and brightens the path of all who truly seek Him. His love, received into the heart, will spring up in good works unto eternal life. And not only does it bless the soul in which it springs, but the living stream will flow out in words and deeds of righteousness, to refresh the thirsting around him.

"The same figure Christ had employed in His conversation with the woman of Samaria at Jacob's well: 'Whosoever drinketh of the water that I shall give him shall never thirst; but the water that I shall give him shall be in him a well of water springing up into everlasting life.' John 4:14. Christ combines the two types. He is the rock, He is the living water" (Ellen G. White, *Patriarchs and Prophets*, p. 412).

7. How does the sanctuary message reveal God's true character? (Isa. 14:12–14; Ezek. 28:12–19; Rev. 12:7–9)

    Since war broke out in heaven, Satan has worked to slander God and assassinate His character. The great controversy and the disposition of sin and Satan are fully portrayed and understood through the sanctuary.

8. What event in Christ's ministry especially portrayed His respect for the sanctuary? (Matt. 21:12, 13; John 2:13–16)

    Casting out the money changers who were desecrating the temple by buying and selling.

9. What happened at Christ's death that graphically showed how the earthly sanctuary services had met their fulfillment and would now completely lose their validity? (Matt. 27:45–51)

    When Christ died the temple veil was torn from top to bottom by an unseen hand.

10. What is Christ's relationship with the heavenly sanctuary? (Heb. 7:28–8:6)

    Today He serves as our High Priest in the heavenly sanctuary.

11. The sanctuary message holds the key to understanding the book of Revelation. What do the following passages teach about the heavenly sanctuary?

   a.   Rev. 1:10–20 – The seven candlesticks, like the seven-branched candlestick in the sanctuary, are the seven churches (Rev. 1:20). Here we see Christ walking among the candlesticks (Rev. 2:1), showing His great love and care for His people.

   b.   Rev. 4:1–6 – The prelude to the seven seals reveals God's majestic throne in the heavenly sanctuary, His worthiness as our Creator, and His right to send impending judgments upon the earth.

   c.   Rev. 11:18, 19 – At the end of the seven trumpets, God's temple is opened in heaven and the heavenly ark of the covenant is seen. This shows us that the heavenly sanctuary, so long ignored by humans, will play a significant part in end-time events.

   d.   Rev. 15:1–6 – In this prelude to the seven last plagues of chapter 16, God's judgments emanate from the heavenly temple.

   e.   Rev. 21:22 – Finally, no more temple! All the major lines of prophecy in Revelation emanate from the heavenly sanctuary, and the book itself is full of allusions to it. Thus, Revelation comes alive to those who understand the sanctuary.

Lesson 3

Jesus Predicts the Destruction of the Temple

In our last lesson we saw how the sanctuary portrays the most basic of Christian doctrines—salvation through the atoning sacrifice of Christ—but that atonement process would not be complete without His second coming, which we will study about in this lesson.

1. The disciples were very proud of the temple. Its gleaming marble façade and beautiful furnishings topped the highest point in Jerusalem. One day when they were giving Jesus a tour of the "buildings of the temple," Jesus made a stunning prediction (Matt. 24:1, 2). A short while later, seated on a nearby hilltop, they confronted Jesus with what question? (Matt. 24:3)

    "Tell us, when will these things be? And what will be the sign of Your coming, and of the end of the age?" They evidently equated such a momentous event with the end of the world.

2. Had the temple ever been destroyed before? Trace this brief history of the Jewish temple:

    a. 2 Sam. 7:1–13 – David wanted to build a temple, but God wouldn't allow it.

    b.   1 Kings 7:51–8:5 – The temple was finally built and dedicated by King Solomon.

    c.   2 Chron. 36:15–21 – Because of Israel's unfaithfulness, the temple was destroyed by the Babylonians in 586 BC.

    d.   Ezra 3:10–13 – The temple was rebuilt after seventy years in Babylonian captivity, and later it was completely refurbished and enlarged under King Herod the Great.

3.   We saw Jesus' great respect for the temple in our previous lesson, yet because the Jews as a whole rejected their Messiah, the temple was doomed again. Matthew 23 contains a series of "woes" against the scribes and Pharisees. What does Jesus say about Jerusalem in verses 37–39?

    He said that their house would be left desolate. In other words, Israel as a nation would never again be God's chosen nation, even though individual Israelites would certainly be welcomed into the new, spiritual Israel, the Christian church.

4.   What were the two parts to the disciples' question in Matthew 24:3? And what was Jesus' response in the subsequent verses?

    Jesus' response mingles both the destruction of Jerusalem and the end of world—one event in their minds, but in reality, two separate events. This exemplifies the dual-fulfillment principle that applies to many prophecies.

One account of the terrible destruction that occurred in AD 70 under the Roman general Titus reads as follows: "The blind obstinacy of the Jewish leaders, and the detestable crimes perpetrated within the besieged city, excited the horror and indignation of the Romans, and Titus at last decided to take the temple by storm. He determined, however, that if possible it should be saved from destruction. But his commands were disregarded. After he had retired to his tent at night, the Jews, sallying from the temple, attacked the soldiers without. In the struggle, a firebrand was flung by a soldier through an opening in the porch, and immediately the cedar-lined chambers about the holy house were in a blaze. Titus rushed to the place, followed by his generals and legionaries, and commanded the soldiers to quench the flames. His words were unheeded. In their fury the soldiers hurled blazing brands into the chambers adjoining the temple, and then with their swords they slaughtered in great numbers those who had found shelter there. Blood flowed down the temple steps like water. Thousands upon thousands of Jews perished. Above the sound of battle, voices were heard shouting: 'Ichabod!'—the glory is departed" (Ellen G. White, *The Great Controversy*, p. 33).

5. As you read Matthew 24, how many of the signs apply to either the destruction of Jerusalem or Christ's second coming, or both events?

    Many of these signs would occur in connection with both events. For example, we know of several false messiahs that arose prior to the destruction of Jerusalem, and Paul said in Colossians 1:23 that the gospel had been preached to the whole world in his day, at least the world that he was aware of.

6. What solemn warning did Jesus give us toward the end of His discourse in Matthew 24? (verse 44)

    He warned them to always be ready.

7. Several parables about "being ready" are found in Matthew 22 and 25. What lessons do they bring forth?

    a. The wedding feast (Matt. 22:1–14) – We are to accept the wedding garment, righteousness by faith.

    b. The wise and foolish virgins (Matt. 25:1–13) – We need the "oil" of the Holy Spirit to prepare us for the Bridegroom's return.

    c. The talents (Matt. 25:14–30) – The importance of

"investing" ourselves in serving God. When we do, He blesses us with more talents.

d.   The judgment (Matt. 25:31–46) – Our works of compassion and charity are noted in heaven.

> Note that according to several of Jesus' parables, the separation of the wicked and the righteous occurs only at the end of the world, and not at death (Matt. 13:24–30, 38–43; Matt. 13:47–50; Matt. 25:31–33).

8.   How does the Bible describe Christ's second coming? (1 Thess. 4:13–18; 1 Cor. 15:51–54)

Scripture describes the second coming as a literal, visible coming in which every eye will see Him. There will not be a secret rapture.

9.   What does "as a thief in the night" mean? (1 Thess. 5:2; 2 Peter 3:10)

When He returns, Jesus takes the world by surprise.

10.   God has promised us a new earth where we will be free at last from Satan and sin. What characteristics distinguish God's kingdom, which we will enjoy for eternity? (Rev. 21:4)

There will be no death, crying, or sorrow in heaven. It makes no sense to imagine that the new earth would be any other way. With Satan, sin, and sinners completely eradicated, we will be free at last!

Lesson 4

The Covenant of the Ark

There is a great deal of misunderstanding in the Christian world in regard to God's covenants with His people. This lesson will explore the Bible for important insight into the new covenant.

1. The ark in the sanctuary/tabernacle/temple was called "the ark of the covenant." This term is found forty-six times in the New King James Version Bible according to BibleGateway.com. Whose ark was it? (Num. 10:33; Josh. 3:11)

   It was the ark of the Lord of all the earth.

> Notice that when "Lord" is spelled with three small capital letters at the end (LORD), it is in place of "Jehovah" or "Jahweh" in the original Hebrew.

2. In general terms, what is a covenant? (Gen. 9:12–17)

   "Covenant" is a relational term. It is an agreement between two or more parties, with stated terms. Marriage is a covenant, as are sales agreements, treaties between warring parties, contracts of various kinds, etc. In this case, God made an agreement to save His people.

3. What do we call God's covenant with humanity? (Heb. 13:20)
    God's everlasting covenant of love.

4. Why was the ark called "the ark of the covenant"? (Exod. 34:28)
    Because it contained the words of the covenant, God's law as
    written in the Ten Commandments, and the mercy seat.

5. There are many covenants in the Bible, but in this study we will
    focus on those covenants that have a bearing on our salvation.
    What can we learn from the following covenants?

    a. The "old covenant" between God and man (Gen. 2:16, 17)
        – The covenant in the Garden of Eden was obey and live,
        disobey and die.

    b. The "new covenant" after they sinned (Gen. 3:15) – After
        the fall, the "new covenant" was the promise of a Savior.

    c. A trial run of the old covenant (Exod. 19:4–8; 24:3–7) –
        When the Israelites were released from Egypt, God called
        them to obedience and a life of purity in following Him.
        However, it didn't take long for them to break the covenant
        and turn to a god they could see (Exod. 32:19).

    d. The new covenant, enshrined in the ark (Exod. 25:8–22) –
        Especially note verses 16 and 21, which deal with the law
        and the mercy seat.

6. The two eternal principles of God's character and kingdom are
    perfect justice (based on law) and perfect mercy. What are some
    major events of Bible history that trace these coexisting principles?

    a. Gen. 3:7, 21 – Fig leaves versus animal skins

    b. Gen. 4:3–5 – Man's efforts versus acts of faith

    c. Gen. 22:7–14 – Abraham's supreme test, and the principle of substitutionary atonement

d. Exod. 29:38, 39; Lev. 1:1–5 – The sacrificial system as a part of the sanctuary services

e. Matt. 27:46–51 – The death of Jesus, the Lamb of God

7. What beautiful covenant term is used in the Bible to describe one's Christian relationship with the Savior?

a. Isa. 54:5 – God is our maker and our husband.

b. Rev. 21:9, 10 – We are Christ's bride.

c. Eph. 5:22–32 – The marriage relationship is a symbol of our union with Christ.

8. Were people in the Old Testament saved any differently than in the New Testament? (Isa. 55:6, 7; Ps. 51)

Many struggle with the concept of works versus faith, law versus grace, etc., but the fact remains that there is no other way to be saved than by grace! People on both sides of the cross have attempted salvation by their works, whether good deeds or religious rituals, but our works are never good enough! Only the blood of Jesus can save.

9. What are the important distinctions between the Ten Commandment law and the ceremonial law?

a. The Ten Commandments (Exod. 25:16, 21; 31:18; 40:20; Deut. 9:10) – The Ten Commandments were written by God's own finger on tables of stone and placed in the ark.

b. The ceremonial law (Deut. 31:26) – The ceremonial law was written on scrolls and placed alongside the ark.

10. Is the ceremonial law still applicable? (Heb. 9:9–12; Col. 2:14;

Eph. 2:15; Heb. 10:1)

The "law of Moses" contains many ordinances regarding civil life, marriage, health, etc., many of which are timeless and still of value, but they have only an indirect bearing on our salvation. Those laws pertaining to the ceremonies that prefigured the death of Jesus ceased to have validity when Christ died.

11. Is the moral law, the Ten Commandments, still applicable? (Ps. 19:7; Isa. 42:21; Matt. 5:18; Rom. 7:12; 3:31)

The moral principles of the Ten Commandments are timeless. They are the very character of God expressed as laws. Without them we would have no guidance regarding our human behavior. Adhering to them, with the help of Christ, is our goal. And when we fail, we have a Savior who is ready to forgive us and point us in the right direction! If we were to abolish this law, we have no need for a Savior at all, and no basis for the final judgment.

12. What principles of the new covenant are important for us today?

   a.   Jer. 31:31–34; Ezek. 36:26, 27 – God wants to write it in our hearts.

   b.   Luke 22:20 – The Lord's supper reminds us of the new covenant whenever we observe it.

   c.   Heb. 8:1–6; Rev. 11:15–19 – Jesus is now the Mediator of the new covenant.

13. What must I do to begin my journey with Christ and enter into a covenant relationship with Him? (Acts 16:31; Rom. 10:9; Col. 2:12; Gal. 3:27)

We must believe in God and confess our sins in order to accept His gift of salvation. We then may be baptized as a public display of our commitment to dying to self and living for God.

Lesson 5

The Ark's Environment

The ark of the covenant was only one feature of the sanctuary. This lesson focuses on the other articles of furniture and their significance. God, who designed the sanctuary in the first place, gave each item deep meaning. The sanctuary, after all, was not a church or place of assembly as we think of today, but as was mentioned in lesson 2, the sanctuary was a divinely appointed visual aid, whose purpose was to portray various facets of His character of love and His plan to save fallen humanity.

1. Where did the design for the first sanctuary, or tabernacle, come from? (Exod. 25:1–9; 26:30)

   God gave a detailed design to Moses, and Moses directed the construction. Our "invisible" God needed some visibility among the people for their own benefit (Exod. 29:42, 43). Many religions have had their counterfeit temples and rituals, and the Israelites were no different. Many turned the benefit of being able to meet with God into a focus on the rituals.

2. Do you notice anything unique in Paul's overview of the tabernacle in Hebrews 9:1–10? (see also Exod. 31:1–11)

   Notice the word "symbolic" in verse 9. It was meant to be temporary "until the time of reformation." Not only the sanctuary and its furniture, but every service and ritual conducted there was a prophecy of future events in the plan of salvation.

3. God is a God of detail. There was not a single element of the
    sanctuary left to the workers' imaginations. What are some of the
    features you notice in each of the areas?

    a. The courtyard (Exod. 27:9–19) – It was defined on all sides
        by beautiful curtains in a framework of brass and silver
        hangings. It is helpful to read the verses in this question in
        the New International Version. Also, note that there was a
        very special reason why the entrance to the sanctuary was
        always on the east. It was so that the people would enter in
        the morning with their backs to the sun, the exact opposite
        of the pagan temples where sun worship was practiced.

    b. The tabernacle itself (Exod. 26) – The tabernacle itself was
        also formed by beautiful curtains and animal skins, both
        around and above, as well as framing of acacia wood.

    c. The veil (Exod. 26:31–35; 30:6) – The veil separated the
        Holy Place from the Most Holy Place, and special care was
        taken to embroider it with the figures of angels.

    d. The altar of burnt offering (Exod. 27:1–8) – The altar of
        burnt offering was in the courtyard and was the location for
        the animal sacrifices that were offered.

    e. The laver (Exod. 30:17–21) – The laver was a place of
        washing for the priests before they entered the Holy Place.

f.   The table of showbread (Exod. 25:23–30) – This was a table made from acacia wood and overlaid with gold, whereon the special unleavened bread was placed each day.

g.   The gold lampstand (Exod. 25:31–40) – There are seven candlesticks, not nine like the present-day Jewish menorah.

h.   The altar of incense (Exod. 30:1–10) – Although the altar of incense was physically in the Holy Place, it was considered to be part of the Most Holy Place (see Heb. 9:3, 4).

i.   The ark of the covenant (Exod. 25:10–22) – The lesson from the ark is that justice and mercy are perfectly blended.

j.   The priestly garments (Exod. 28, especially verses 29, 30) – The priest was outfitted in a way that represented the people to God, and God to the people.

4.   Let's now "enter" the sanctuary. How did the following things point forward to Jesus?

a.   The altar of burnt offering (John 1:29; Heb. 7:25–27; 9:12) – Jesus would be the sacrifice.

b.   The gold lampstand (John 8:12) – Jesus is the Light of the World.

   c.   The table of showbread (John 6:41–51) – Jesus is the Bread of Life.

   d.   The priest (Heb. 8:1, 2; 9:11, 12, 24) – Jesus was both the sacrifice and the priest.

5.   Two major types of sacrifices were offered at the sanctuary. What were they?

   a.   Exod. 29:38–46 – The morning and evening sacrifices for the congregation as a whole.

   b.   Lev. 4:1–6 – The individual sinner could bring a sacrifice.

6.   Six special holy convocations or "feasts" were observed throughout the calendar year, three in the spring and three in the fall. What did they signify?

   a.   The Passover and Unleavened Bread (Lev. 23:4–8; 1 Cor. 5:7) – Christ's death

   b.   The Feast of Firstfruits (Harvest) (Lev. 23:9–14; Matt. 27:50–53) – Christ's resurrection

   c.   The Feast of Weeks/Pentecost (Lev. 23:15–22; Acts 2:1–4) – The coming of the Holy Spirit

   d.   The Feast of Trumpets (Lev. 23:23–25) – Preparation for judgment

    e.   The Day of Atonement (Lev. 23:26–32; 16:29, 30) – The judgment day

    f.   The Feast of Tabernacles (Lev. 23:33–44) – Our final deliverance

7. Notice that the weekly Sabbath is mentioned separately in Leviticus 23:3. Why do you think the Sabbath is highlighted on its own?

    The Sabbath is highlighted because the Ten Commandment Sabbath was in no way part of the ceremonial law.

8. As we study the sanctuary, it becomes ever clearer that God is trying to teach us two great salvation principles. What two principles are they?

    a.   God's plan for saving us as individuals.

    b.   God's plan for rescuing planet Earth and restoring His kingdom.

9. How is this portrayed in the overall design of the sanctuary?

    a.   The Holy Place and the "daily" service (Heb. 9:6) – Every day the priest would provide atonement for the individuals as he ministered in the Holy Place.

    b.   The Most Holy Place and the "yearly" service (Heb. 9:7) – Once each year on the Day of Atonement the high priest would officiate in a pageant that represented the final disposition of sin and Satan. We will study this in detail in the next lesson.

10. What important lesson can be learned from the sanctuary, especially from the golden lampstand? (Ps. 119:105)

    Pray that you will always allow God's Word to be your lamp, lighting the pathway of your life, until Jesus comes!

The Earthly Sanctuary

"The sanctuary was and is both pageant and prophecy."

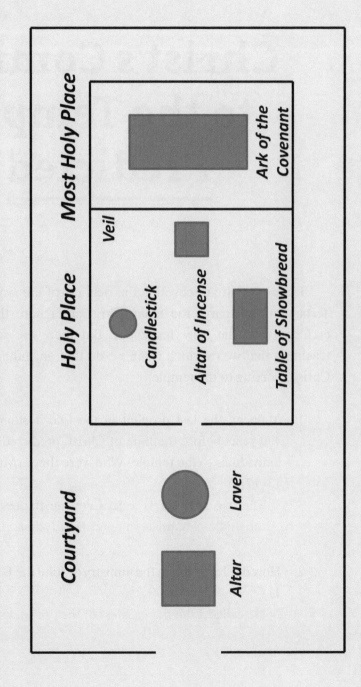

Lesson 6

Christ's Coming to the Temple Predicted

I hope you are discovering the richness of the symbolism in the Old Testament sanctuary. Too many Christians ignore this part and focus exclusively on the New Testament. But there are so many wonderful teachings that we overlook when we do that, including the prediction of Christ's coming to the temple.

1. Malachi, the last prophet in the Old Testament, writing about 400 years before the time of Christ, predicted the coming of two individuals to the temple. Who were they? (Mal. 3:1; Matt. 3:1–3, 13–17)

    The two individuals were John the Baptist and Jesus. Notice the mode of baptism in regards to John and Jesus.

2. How did Jesus affirm the ministry of John the Baptist? (Matt. 11:7–11)

    He called John the greatest of the prophets.

3. What prophecy of Malachi did Jesus link to John the Baptist? (Mal. 4:5, 6; John 1:19–23; Matt. 11:12–14)

    Many Bible scholars believe that Malachi 4:5, 6 was only partially fulfilled because of the words "before the coming of the great and dreadful day of the Lord." There remains an "Elijah message" for our day.

4. Did Jesus come to earth at a particular time in history? (Gal. 4:4, 5; Mark 1:14, 15)

    Absolutely! God is a God of order and design. Nothing takes Him by surprise.

5. The Bible contains a few prophecies that are linked to a particular time, and we are now going to look at one of them. What precedent do we have for interpreting the time factor a certain way? (Ezek. 4:1–6)

    It helps to remember here that the nation, because of civil war centuries before, had split into two parts—Judah and Israel. Israel was the northern kingdom, and because of their apostasy, God allowed them to be invaded and destroyed by Assyria in 722 BC. Judah was besieged by the Babylonians in 605 BC, and its people sent into exile (see also Num. 14:34).

6. This, then, is the "day for a year" principle, which can safely be applied to many time prophecies. Daniel was one of those exiles, who distinguished himself in that setting and was elevated to leadership in the Babylonian government, and later in the successor government of Persia. What is the sequence of events outlined in Daniel 9?

    a. Dan. 9:1, 2; Jer. 25:11, 12 – Daniel acknowledged the inspired writings of Jeremiah, who had remained behind in the homeland, that the seventy-year captivity was going to end soon.

b.   **Dan 9:3–19** – He fasted and prayed that the Lord would somehow fulfill His word.

c.   **Dan 9:20–23** – The angel Gabriel came to comfort him and enlighten him regarding "the vision," referring to Daniel's vision as recorded in chapter 8. We will study that vision in our next lesson.

7.   As we unpack the significance of Gabriel's words in Daniel 9, we see a time prophecy that accurately predicted Christ's first coming. If our time prophecy ruler holds true, that a prophetic "day" equals a literal year, how many years would the seventy-weeks prophecy signify? And what do the phrases "are determined" and "for your people" mean? (Dan. 9:24)

The total number of years was 490—the Jews' probationary time. "Are determined" literally means "are cut off." And the phrase "for your people" is referring to the Jews, who were "Daniel's people."

8.   What were they supposed to accomplish during the seventy-weeks period? Did they succeed? (Dan. 9:24; Matt. 23:37–39)

They were supposed to turn their lives around and accept Jesus as the promised Messiah. The language used here by Christ was the language of divorce, which was well known to the Jews.

9.   What event signaled the beginning of the prophecy? (Dan. 9:25)

In 457 BC, King Artaxerxes of Persia issued a decree that restored the Jews to their homeland and financed the reconstruction of Jerusalem.

10. Do we have a copy of this decree that was the catalyst for the prophecy? (Ezra 7:11–26)

> There had been other decrees, but this one was financially backed by King Artaxerxes.

11. When was the Messiah, Jesus, supposed to come to His temple? (Dan. 9:26)

> He was to arrive after sixty-nine weeks.

12. What would happen to the temple some years after Christ's death? (Matt. 24:1, 2, 15–20)

> It would be destroyed by the Romans.

13. How would Christ "confirm a covenant for one week" with the Jews? (Matt. 10:5, 6; Acts 13:42–46)

> For seven years the Jews were the target of the gospel message. This encompassed three and a half years of Jesus' ministry followed by three and a half years of the apostles' ministry. After that, although the Jews could still accept Christ's gift of salvation individually, the apostles focused their efforts on the Gentiles.

14. Was God's covenant with Israel conditional or unconditional? (Deut. 28:1, 2, 15, 16)

> It was conditional.

15. Exactly when did Christ die on Calvary? (Dan. 9:27)

> He died in AD 31 in the midst of the "week" of the Passover.

16. What event showed that the temple sacrifices were abolished, at least in God's eyes? (Matt. 27:51)

> "The veil of the temple was torn in two from top to bottom."

17. Who are God's people today? (Gal. 6:15, 16; 3:27–29; Rom. 9:6–
    8; 11:5, 13–17, 26)

    All those who believe in God and keep His commandments are
    His people.

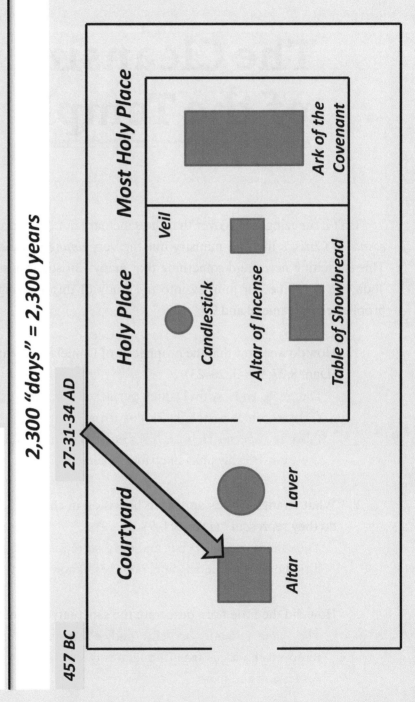

"In the middle of the week He shall bring an end to sacrifice and offering." – Dan. 9:27

70 "weeks" = 490 years

2,300 "days" = 2,300 years

457 BC

27-31-34 AD

Courtyard

Laver

Altar

Holy Place

Most Holy Place

Veil

Candlestick

Altar of Incense

Table of Showbread

Ark of the Covenant

The Cleansing of the Temple

Isn't it amazing to discover that the sanctuary not only portrayed the *events* in Christ's life and ministry but the very *timing* of those events? This is exciting news, and something that many Christians miss entirely. Today we continue our journey into the study of this amazing timeline prophesied in Daniel 8 and 9.

1. How do we know that the prophecies of Daniel 8 and 9 are linked? (Dan. 8:27; 9:1–3, 20–23)

    Daniel 8 ends with Daniel perplexed and confused. Then Gabriel comes to enlighten him at the beginning of Daniel 9. Also, the special Hebrew term *mareh* (vision), which Gabriel uses, inextricably links the two chapters.

2. What strange figures appear in his vision in chapter 8, and what do they represent? (Dan. 8:1–9)

    The ram represents Persia and the goat represents Greece. The little horn represents Rome, otherwise known as the papacy.

3. How did the little horn desecrate the sanctuary? (Dan. 8:10–12)

    The papacy made boastful and blasphemous claims and removed the focus from the heavenly sanctuary by instituting confession and mass.

4. How long would it be until the sanctuary truth was restored? (Dan. 8:13, 14)

   It was to be restored in 2,300 prophetic days, which equals 2,300 years.

5. When did that period begin? (Dan. 9:25)

   It began in 457 BC. In other words, the seventy weeks determined for the Jews was "cut off" from the 2,300 days.

6. The term "cleansing of the sanctuary" was well understood by the Jews to refer to the Day of Atonement, which in turn signified the judgment. Once a year this pageant was re-enacted in a ceremony that focused on the Most Holy Place. What did this ceremony signify? (Lev. 23:26–32; 16:29, 30)

   This ceremony signified the atoning death of Christ (the Lord's goat), the rolling back of sin on the head of the perpetrator, Satan (the scapegoat or Azazel), and his banishment and death.

7. The sanctuary ceremonies are divided into two basic parts: the "daily" and the "yearly" services. What was represented by the daily services? (Mark 15:33–39)

   Christ's death for our sins and His heavenly ministry.

8. So if the daily service is prophetic, what then does the yearly service foretell? (Rev. 20:11–15)

   The yearly service foretold the final judgment and disposition of sin and Satan, the bringing of the great controversy to its end, and the complete restoration of the earth and the universe.

9. Notice Daniel's prophecy of the judgment. What takes place before Christ returns to the earth? (Dan. 7:9, 10)

    The judgment must be completed before Christ returns, because He is bringing His rewards with Him.

10. What solemn sanctuary ceremony portrays God's saving grace? (Lev. 16:7–10)

    The Day of Atonement was an active portrayal of the plan of redemption.

    a. Whom does the Lord's goat represent? Jesus

    b. Whom does the scapegoat (Azazel) represent? Satan

    c. When does the Lord's goat die? (Lev. 16:8, 9; John 19:28–30) – The goat representing Jesus died on the cross for our sins.

    d. When does the scapegoat die? (Lev. 16:10; Rev. 20:7–10) – The scapegoat was banished to the wilderness as a portrayal of when Satan will be left on the desolate earth during the millennium, when the saints are in heaven with Jesus. Satan does not die until after the millennium (see also Ezek. 28:18, 19).

11. Some believe that both goats represent Christ. If both goats had to be perfect, how can we say that Azazel represents Satan? (Ezek. 28:12–15)

    Satan used to be perfect before he rebelled against God's law of love and chose his own path.

12. In what sense is "atonement" used in Leviticus 16:15–22?

    "Atonement" means "making all things right." There are three distinct phases of this portrayed here: (1) my personal atonement as I look back on Christ's sacrifice and ask for forgiveness and pardon; (2) my personal exoneration at the judgment day; (3) the complete riddance of sin and Satan and the restoration of God's universe. Never, ever, will sin rise again. That is great news, and that is atonement in its fullest sense.

13. What happened in 1844 that makes it a significant time in Bible prophecy? (Rev. 10:8–11)

> The "little book" prophesied in Revelation 10 was undoubtedly the book of Daniel. Its message regarding the "cleansing of the sanctuary" was thought to be the second coming of Christ, and thus early believers "sweetly" expected Him to return in 1844. The "great disappointment" turned their hopes into bitterness until they understood the truth of the sanctuary. Further information about this event is located in the sidebars in lesson 12.

Following the symbolism of the sanctuary to its logical conclusion, we believe that part of the judgment began in 1844. We call it the "investigative judgment" because Christ is preparing us for His coming. There is a definite sense in which we, too, should "afflict our souls" as the Israelites did on the Day of Atonement by taking life seriously and living for Jesus.

14. Will we ever have to deal with sin again? (Nahum 1:9)

> No. At the end of the millennium, God will destroy Satan, sin, and sinners once and for all.

"For two thousand three hundred days; then the sanctuary shall be cleansed." – Dan. 8:14

70 "weeks" = 490 years

1810 years

2,300 "days" = 2,300 years

457 BC

27-31-34 AD

1844 AD

Courtyard

Holy Place

Most Holy Place

Altar

Laver

Candlestick

Altar of Incense

Table of Showbread

Veil

Ark of the Covenant

Lesson 8

The Contents of the Ark

In lesson 1 we briefly referred to the contents of the ark of the covenant, but today we are going to look at their deeper significance. This ark was the holiest item in the sanctuary because it represented the very presence of God.

1. How was the ark to be constructed?

    a.   What was its size? (Exod. 25:10) – About 45 x 27 x 27 inches

    b.   What was it made out of? (verses 10, 11) – Acacia wood overlaid with gold inside and out

    c.   How was it to be transported? (verses 12–15) – Using long poles placed in rings

    d.   What went inside the ark? (verse 16) – The Ten Commandments

    e.   What was placed on top of the ark? (verses 17–21) – The mercy seat and the cherubim

    f.   What activity was to take place in front of the ark? (verse 22) – God would meet with Moses

2. What other items would later be added to the ark? (Heb. 9:4; Exod. 16:33, 34; Num. 17:1–10)

    A pot of manna and Aaron's rod were later added to the ark.

3. What do the following items represent in relation to God and His character?

    a.   The Ten Commandments – Holiness, purity, justice, law

    b.   The manna – Providence, goodness

    c.   Aaron's rod – Authority

    d.   The mercy seat – Mercy, grace, forgiveness, love

    e.   The cherubim – Worship, reverence

4. Why is it important for us to have a true picture of God? (Isa. 14:12–15)

    The whole focus of the "great controversy" is on God's character and whether He is true to His word. Satan wants nothing more than to defame God's character and have us believe his lies, that God is unfair and a vengeful God.

We have all heard statements like, "If there is a God, He would not permit ..." Satan takes great delight in these assaults on God's character. The truth is that God is the healer and deliverer, and Satan the destroyer and warmonger.

5. What insight does Jesus' statement to the disciples give us about the blind man and his suffering? (John 9:1–5)

    It tells us that God does not punish for sin by sending sickness or calamity. It is true, however, that sometimes our sins have physical or other consequences.

6. What did the apostle Paul say about his struggle with infirmity and the role Satan played? (2 Cor. 12:7–10)

    He said that it was Satan who caused his personal affliction, not God. He went on to say that God sometimes uses these afflictions to teach us important character traits such as humility, dependence, patience, etc.

7. What does the story of Job teach us about Satan's involvement on this earth? (Job 1:6–12)

    The story of Job teaches us that his problems and trials were caused directly by Satan.

> If God were to suddenly wipe out all of earth's misery, poverty, disease, and death, we would not look forward to heaven. And if God healed only Christians, then many would become a Christian for the wrong reason.

8. Returning to the ark, what are the two basic salvation principles that it teaches us?

    a. The Ten Commandments (Rev. 14:12; 22:14; Matt. 5:17, 18; Rom. 3:20, 31; 7:12) – The commandments are ten eternal moral principles or laws that describe God's character of righteousness and justice and by which we are required, with His help, to live.

    b. The mercy seat (Rom. 3:23, 24; 5:1; James 2:10–12; 1 John 1:9) – This signifies God's grace and forgiveness. He gives us power over the penalty of sin, and power to live victoriously over sin.

9. How did God present Himself to Moses? What character traits did God use to describe Himself? (Exod. 34:5, 6; Ps. 85:10)

    He appeared in a pillar of cloud and called Himself "the Lord." He described Himself as merciful and gracious, longsuffering, abundant in goodness and truth—a perfect blend.

10. What other important characteristic of God is highlighted in the Bible? (Ps. 115:1–8)

    His power to create and the uselessness of false gods.

11. Is there anything in the ark of the covenant that alludes to God as our Creator? (Exod. 20:8–11).

    The fourth commandment, in the very heart of the ten, plainly describes God as Creator and calls us to worship on the day He set aside in the very beginning as an acknowledgement of His authority as Creator of the universe.

12. What do the following texts teach us about the Sabbath day?

    a. Gen. 2:1–3 – An important point of this verse is that this was set in stone thousands of years before the Jews were a people group.

    b. Mark 2:27, 28 – Jesus, our Creator, affirmed that He is Lord of the Sabbath.

    c. Exod. 16:23–29 – The Sabbath was known to the Jews before the law was given in Exodus 20.

    d. Neh. 13:15–22 – Nehemiah championed the Sabbath during the return of the Jews.

    e. Acts 13:42–44; 16:13 – Paul observed the Sabbath, even among the Gentiles.

    f.   Heb. 4:8, 9 – The book of Hebrews affirmed Sabbath keeping late in the first century.

    g.   Isa. 66:22, 23 – We will even keep the Sabbath in the new earth!

13. If keeping the law doesn't actually save us, what good is the law, and do we need to follow it? (James 1:22–25; Rom. 3:20)

    The law is like a mirror. It reveals our sin and drives us to the cross to obtain forgiveness. Without the law we would have no way to distinguish between sin and righteousness.

> "The precious record of the law was placed in the ark of the testament and is still there, safely hidden from the human family. But in God's appointed time He will bring forth these tables of stone to be a testimony to all the world against the disregard of His commandments and against the idolatrous worship of a counterfeit Sabbath" (Ellen G. White, *Manuscript Releases*, vol. 8, p. 100).

Lesson 9

Parables of the Kingdom

The people of Jesus' day, including His own disciples, had some very twisted notions in regard to the kingdom of God. They were looking for a Messiah who would overthrow the oppressive Romans and restore the nation to earthly greatness. In this lesson we will explore the parables that Jesus told as He patiently explained the true nature of His kingdom and the final events that would usher it in.

1. What do the following parables of Jesus teach us about the *timing* of the day of judgment?

   a. The wheat and tares (Matt. 13:24–30, 36–43)

   b. The dragnet (Matt. 13:47–50)

   c. The final judgment (Matt. 25:31–34, 41)
      All of these parables point to the judgment, which occurs at the end of the world when Christ returns. Then, and only then, does the separation of the righteous from the wicked occur. Therefore, it is impossible that this separation takes place at death. It also gives us insight into God's fairness, that the eternal reward or punishment is given to everyone at the same time. How could someone go to heaven or hell before they are judged?

2. What can we learn from the following supporting scriptures?

    a. Dan. 7:9, 10 – There is definitely a day of judgment.

    b. Acts 24:15 – The judgment occurs at the resurrection. Note
        verse 25 and Felix's reaction.

    c. Mark 13:24–27 – Jesus plainly teaches that the righteous are
        not gathered until His coming.

    d. John 5:28, 29 – The resurrection occurs at a particular point
        in time, referred to as the "hour."

    e. Acts 2:29–35 – Even King David is dead and buried in
        the ground, awaiting Christ's second coming and the
        resurrection of the righteous.

    f. 1 Cor. 15:51–54; 1 Thess. 4:13–17 – Paul graphically
        portrays the resurrection at the second coming.

3. In lesson 7 we learned that a facet of the judgment began in the
    year 1844. What does this entail? (Dan. 7:9, 10)
        Judgment generally occurs in distinct phases: (1) trial; (2) verdict;
        (3) sentencing; (4) execution. Therefore, we believe that the "trial
        phase" began in 1844. We call it the "investigative judgment." It is
        a very important part of the preparation for Christ's coming.

4. When does the verdict phase occur? (2 Thess. 2:8; Rev. 6:15–17)
        That phase takes place at Christ's second coming.

5. Is that it for the wicked? What is the sequence of events outlined
    in Revelation 19 and 20?

    a. Rev. 19:11–16 – Christ will return to earth.

    b. Rev. 19:17–21 – The wicked will die at the brightness of His
        appearing.

c.   Rev. 20:1–3 – Satan will be bound for 1,000 years.

d.   Rev. 20:4–6; 1 Cor. 6:2, 3 – The saved will be involved in a form of judgment during the millennium in heaven.

e.   Rev. 20:7–14 – The wicked will be raised, sentenced, and destroyed along with Satan.

6.   The whole book of Revelation is bathed in sanctuary language. What do you notice in the following passages?

a.   Rev. 1:9–20 – The preamble to the prophecy of the seven churches

b.   Rev. 4 – The preamble to the prophecy of the seven seals

c.   Rev. 8:1–6 – The preamble to the prophecy of the seven trumpets

d.   Rev. 11:1–3 – The preamble to the prophecy of the two witnesses

e.   Rev. 15:5–8 – The preamble to the prophecy of the seven plagues
All of these lines of prophecy begin in the heavenly sanctuary. There is mention of the golden candlesticks, God's throne, angels, an altar of incense, the courtyard, etc.

7.   What event is described in Revelation 14:14–16?
Christ's second coming is described in this passage.

8.   Does God seek to catch us off guard with His coming, or does He give us forewarning? (Matt. 24:25; Jonah 3:1–4)
God always warns His people of impending judgment.

9.   How does God warn the world just prior to Christ's coming? (Rev. 14:6–13)

God sends three angels with three messages to warn His people. This is what Seventh-day Adventists refer to as the "three angels' messages." There is no other denomination that teaches this!

10. We now examine the three angels' messages in some detail. What are the components of the first angel's message? (Rev. 14:6, 7)

   a. Flying in the midst of heaven – This is an extremely urgent, important message.
   b. The everlasting gospel – This refers to the full gospel, the whole story from beginning to end.
   c. To every nation – This is a universal message, which is meant for everyone, everywhere.
   d. Fear God, give Him glory – The messages are Christ-centered, not humanistic.
   e. The hour of judgment – Now is the time to get ready, not later.
   f. Worship the Creator – This speaks to God's creative power and proves His authority (Ps. 115:1–8).

11. What do we learn about the second angel's message? (Rev. 14:8; see also Rev. 17 and 18, especially 18:1–4)

   We read about the fall of "Babylon," which stands for those who oppose God and His people.

12. What does the third angel's message proclaim? (Rev. 14:9–11)

   It proclaims the mark of the beast and the destruction of the wicked. God seals His people in Revelation 14:1 and marks the wicked.

13. In direct contrast to the wicked in Babylon, how are the righteous described just before Christ's coming? (Rev. 14:12, 13)

   The righteous will reflect God's character, a perfect blending of law and grace, works and faith—just like the ark of the covenant!

Lesson 10

Holiness to the Lord

When the people of Israel were freed from hundreds of years of enslavement in the land of Egypt, to a great degree they had lost their faith and had to be completely re-educated in the things of the Lord and in basic life principles. Notable exceptions would include Moses' parents and a handful of faithful Israelites, for we know that God has always preserved His truth throughout history, even if it often went underground. Once the Israelites set up camp in the wilderness, it was no longer practical for each family to individually practice the sacrificial rituals at home, so the sanctuary system was introduced. This lesson focuses on the concept of holiness.

1. What visible sign of holiness was part of the priest's garment? (Exod. 28:36–38; 39:30, 31)

    The words "holiness to the Lord" were inscribed on their garment.

2. What does it mean to be "holy"? (1 Peter 1:16; Matt. 5:48)

    To be holy means to be set apart, sanctified, righteous, perfect. In one sense, holiness is an unattainable goal for a human being; in another, it is totally achievable when by God's grace we are forgiven.

3. How did God begin to reveal His plan of holiness to the people through Moses? (Exod. 3:1–5)

    Remember, the people can rise no higher than their leader. Sanctified leadership is crucial.

4. How did God set forth this ideal before the people as a whole? (Exod. 19:3–6; 20:8)

> They were to be a kingdom of priests. They were to be an example for the nations around them and bring other people to the Lord. They were not to become some exclusive club. The Sabbath was to remind them of their need of holiness, laying aside personal pursuits for one day each week.

5. What experience on the journey to Canaan underlined the urgency of the concept of holiness? (Lev. 10:1–10)

> Aaron's sons disregarded the sanctity of their position. God had to make a graphic example of Nadab and Abihu in order to show the people the seriousness of holiness (especially see verse 10).

6. In what other way was holiness to be reflected in their lifestyle? (Lev. 11:44–47; Acts 10:9–16, 28)

> These words come at the end of a whole chapter on the subject of diet. As you study the other "laws of Moses," you will find all kinds of areas discussed: camp sanitation, disposal of the dead, how to deal with leprosy and other diseases, etc. In each example it uses the terms "clean" and "unclean."

7. God challenges us to achieve holiness in every area of our lives, such as:

a. 1 Cor. 3:16 – Our lifestyle in general

b. 1 Cor. 6:9–11 – Our sexual powers

c. Lev. 27:30; Mal. 3:8–10 – Our money

8. The concept of holiness is carried throughout the Bible. What can we learn about this concept in the Old and New Testaments? (Ezek. 22:26; 44:16–23; 1 Peter 2:9)

    God always holds high the standard of holiness. He doesn't do this to discourage us but to cause us to depend on Him. His perfect ideal for us is for our good, to bring us peace, wholeness, and true happiness. Consider what would happen if He didn't hold His creation to a high standard.

9. What medieval theology obliterated the "priesthood of the believer" and became an issue in the Protestant Reformation?

    An institutionalized priesthood, mass, indulgences for sin, the veneration of Mary as our mediator, and confession to a priest. Note "altar-centered" versus "pulpit-centered" churches.

10. What happened to the priesthood when Christ died? (Matt. 27:51; Heb. 8:1–6)

    Christ became our only Mediator, our High Priest, in the heavenly sanctuary.

11. In what sense do we serve as "priests" today? (John 21:15–17; 1 Peter 5:3–5)

    Even though these words were addressed to elders, in a very real sense we can all be "under shepherds," as we point people to Christ and engage in intercessory prayer.

12. What postmodern concept has blurred the distinction between the holy and the unholy?

    Relativism has blurred the lines. The idea that "I'm OK; you're OK" and that there aren't any right or wrong answers destroys the biblical ideal of personal holiness and plays directly into Satan's hands. True Christianity is definitely countercultural.

13. What perspective will help us dedicate our lives completely to God? (Heb. 11:13; 1 Peter 2:11)

> Remembering that this world is not our home, as the old song so nicely states.

14. Becoming "holy" is clearly a foreign concept to the world in general. How does the Lord counsel us to put life in perspective and put Him first so that by association with Him we can become holy?

   a. 1 John 2:15–17 – We are not to love the world and its ways.

   b. 2 Peter 3:10–13 – Our focus should be on heavenly things, not on those things that will soon burn up.

Let us all pray that the Lord will do His wonderful work in our lives, and thus prepare us for His heavenly kingdom! "Prayer is heaven's ordained means of success in the conflict with sin and the development of Christian character. The divine influences that come in answer to the prayer of faith will accomplish in the soul of the suppliant all for which he pleads. For the pardon of sin, for the Holy Spirit, for a Christlike temper, for wisdom and strength to do His work, for any gift He has promised, we may ask; and the promise is, 'Ye shall receive'" (Ellen G. White, *The Acts of the Apostles*, p. 564).

Lesson 11

Heavenly Mediation

Especially in today's world, man is considered independent and self-sufficient. "Freedom" for many is interpreted to mean that morally we answer to no one, that we are autonomous. Closely related to that is the idea of relativism—what I believe may differ from what you believe, and we are both right! "Truth" is OK for the mathematician, the physicist, the chemist, etc., but behavioral truth doesn't exist and is conditioned by our culture and upbringing. The sad results of these philosophies are all around us.

1. In the parable of the lost sheep, was the sheep "free"? (Luke 15:3–7)

   He was out of the sheepfold and could roam anywhere he wanted, but he was headed for disaster and didn't know it.

2. What was Jesus' mission while on earth? (Luke 19:10)

   He came to save the lost. We are the lost sheep. Without Jesus we are hopelessly confused and lost.

3. Jesus' mediation began while on earth. For whom did He intercede? (John 17:6–21)

   He prayed for His disciples, and for us!

4. What is the only way to be truly free? (John 17:17; 14:6; 8:30–36)

   The Jews felt they were free, but they weren't. We cannot trust our feelings! We need the Bible and a relationship with the Savior to keep us on the right path.

5. What does the sanctuary teach us about Jesus, our Savior and Mediator?

    a. Heb. 9:12 – Jesus died for us; He was the sacrificial Lamb.

    b. Heb. 8:1, 2, 6 – Jesus lives for us; He is our Mediator.

    c. Heb. 9:28 – Jesus will return to earth to take us to heaven. Notice that He will return for "those who eagerly wait for Him."

6. What qualifies Christ to be our Mediator? (Heb. 4:15, 16; 5:8, 9) He lived a perfect life in this sin-sick world, and He knows from personal experience what it is like to be a human and be tempted, yet to rely fully on God and not fall into sin.

7. What do the following scriptures teach us regarding the mediation of Christ?

    a. 1 Tim. 2:5, 6 – There is only one Mediator—Jesus.

    b. Heb. 8:6; 9:15 – He is the Mediator of the new covenant, a relational agreement that God offers us, by which we may receive salvation.

    c. John 14:1–6 – Jesus is "the way, the truth, and the life." We come to God through Him. This is why we pray "in Jesus' name." See also Acts 2:38; 3:6; 16:18.

> It is important to note that some theological systems point to other "mediators," such as priests, Mary, etc. These erroneous ideas arose during the great apostasy of Christianity after the time of the apostles.

8. If Jesus is mediating for us in the heavenly sanctuary, who is here on earth helping us? (John 16:7) The Holy Spirit; the Comforter that Jesus promised He would

send upon His resurrection and ascension.

9. What is the Holy Spirit's work? (John 16:8–13)

    The Holy Spirit's job is to convict us of sin, righteousness, and judgment, and to lead us into all truth.

10. What qualifies us to benefit from the Holy Spirit's work? (John 14:15–17; Heb. 10:14)

    The disobedient may hear the Spirit's voice calling them to repentance, but only the obedient enjoy a full relationship with Him. Please note that this is not a legalistic obedience but one that springs from the heart, an ongoing process of sanctification that brings us to perfection.

11. How can we find this truth? (John 18:36–38)

    We find truth only through Jesus and His Word. We must surrender our personal concepts of "freedom" and find in Him the only true freedom—a full relationship with Jesus and His Word.

12. What is the Holy Spirit's role when we pray? (Rom. 8:26, 27)

    Here the Holy Spirit is also referred to as an intercessor.

13. How does the Holy Spirit empower us to serve others? (1 Cor. 12:1, 7–11)

    He gives us spiritual gifts.

14. How do Christ and the Holy Spirit open the doors of heaven for us right now? (Eph. 3:12; Heb. 4:16)

    Through prayer we have access to the very throne room of God!

15. All the truths we have studied today emanate from the sanctuary. How did the psalmists express their joy regarding God's house? (Ps. 77:13; 122:1)

They took great delight in going into God's house.

16. What happened in the days of King Josiah when the Scriptures were rediscovered? (2 Kings 22:8–13)

    There was a great revival and reformation.

17. When Huldah the prophetess was consulted, what did she say, especially to the young king? (2 Kings 22:15–20)

    Josiah's sincere repentance was accepted, and the calamities were delayed until after his day.

> May we humble our hearts to receive the Word of God and surrender our lives to Jesus!

Lesson 12

The Ark of Safety

We begin our final lesson with this quote from *The Great Controversy*: "The subject of the sanctuary was the key which unlocked the mystery of the disappointment of 1844. *It opened to view a complete system of truth, connected and harmonious,* showing that God's hand had directed the great advent movement and revealing present duty as it brought to light the position and work of His people" (Ellen G. White, p. 423, emphasis mine).

We could discuss the quest for the earthly ark of the covenant but that would only satisfy a curiosity to solve the mystery of its location. In this final lesson, let's devote our time to studying the heavenly ark, which has been obscured by several layers of false theology through the centuries. Satan succeeded in grand measure in directing mankind's focus away from Christ and to a visible "kingdom" on earth to create a dependency on a church system rather than on the ministry of our heavenly high priest.

1. What earthly system prevailed during the Dark Ages, and what means did it use to draw attention to itself and away from Christ? (Dan. 8:9; Rev. 13:6)

   The little horn prevailed. It usurped the power of Christ, our Mediator in heaven, by instituting a false mediation system on earth that operates a visible church with its priests and "saints" (see. Dan. 8:11, 12).

2. What are the main characteristics that help us identify this power? (Dan. 8:9–13; Rev. 13:1–8)

   The main characteristics are geographical and historical timing, self-exaltation against the Prince of the host, taking away the daily sacrifices and casting down the place of the sanctuary, and casting truth down to the ground.

3. When would this false system be unmasked? (Dan. 8:14; Heb. 9:23)

    The false system was unmasked in the revival of 1844.

"This prophetic period came to its close on October 22, 1844. The disappointment to those who expected to meet their Lord on that day was great. Hiram Edson, a careful Bible student in mid-New York State, describes what took place among the company of believers of which he was a part:

"'Our expectations were raised high, and thus we looked for our coming Lord until the clock tolled twelve at midnight. The day had then passed, and our disappointment had become a certainty. Our fondest hopes and expectations were blasted, and such a spirit of weeping came over us as I never experienced before. It seemed that the loss of all earthly friends could have been no comparison. We wept and wept, till the day dawn....

"'I mused in my heart, saying: "My advent experience has been the brightest of all my Christian experience.... Has the Bible proved a failure? Is there no God, no heaven, no golden city, no Paradise? Is all this but a cunningly devised fable? Is there no reality to our fondest hopes and expectations?"...

"'I began to feel there might be light and help for us in our distress. I said to some of the brethren: "Let us go to the barn." We entered the granary, shut the doors about us, and bowed before the Lord. We prayed earnestly, for we felt our necessity. We continued in earnest prayer until the witness of the Spirit was given that our prayers were accepted, and that light should be given—our disappointment explained, made clear and satisfactory.

"'After breakfast I said to one of my brethren, "Let us go and see and encourage some of our brethren." We started, and while passing through a large field, I was stopped about midway of the field. Heaven seemed open to my view, and I saw distinctly and clearly that instead of our High Priest coming out of the most holy place of the heavenly sanctuary to this earth on the tenth day of the seventh month, at the end of the 2300 days, He, for the first time, entered on that day into the second apartment of that sanctuary, and that He had a work to perform in the most holy place before coming to the earth; that He came to the marriage, or in other words, to the Ancient of Days, to receive a kingdom, dominion, and glory; and that we must wait for His return from the wedding. And my mind was directed to the tenth chapter of Revelation, where I could see the vision had spoken and did not lie'—Unpublished manuscript published in part in The Review and Herald, June 23, 1921" (Ellen G. White, *Christ in His Sanctuary*, p. 5).

4.   Who is the Prince of the host? (Josh. 5:13–15; Dan. 9:25; 10:21; 12:1)

Jesus is the Prince of the host, the very one Satan hates and whose ministry he tried to obscure.

5.   In what specific ways did the little horn's theology succeed in replacing Jesus' ministry?

a.   A wrong priesthood (Rev. 1:6; 1 Peter 2:9) – We are the priests, and Jesus is the High Priest. We can intercede for others through prayer. The earthly priesthood was abolished forever when the temple veil was torn in two.

b.   A false mediatorial system (Heb. 8:1–6) – We are not to pray to dead people such as Mary, St. Jude, etc., nor are we to confess our sins to a priest.

c.   A false religious system with its mystical trappings such as burning incense, statues and icons, an altar-centered and divided chancel, holy water, relics, and other such non-biblical things. – Mass is a total distortion of the communion service. These and many other traditions still linger in Catholic, Orthodox, and Evangelical churches. In summary, we are not to consider the church to be our savior.

> Hebrews 9:24 reveals that the earthly sanctuary and its furnishings were only "copies of the true." Therefore, the real "lost ark" was rediscovered in 1844, in a cornfield, by a dedicated layperson! This ark, the heavenly sanctuary, and the heavenly ministry of Jesus came to light and resulted in a new Christian movement known as the Seventh-day Adventist Church. What are the "secrets and mysteries" of this "lost ark"? They are only secrets and mysteries because most people never study the sanctuary, and so the ark has become lost.
>
> Note: The Seventh-day Adventist Church holds many of its teachings in common with other denominations, but it is the *only* one that teaches the sanctuary message!

6. So in review, and according to what we have discovered through this series of lessons, what are some of the major Bible teachings given to us in the sanctuary message—the "jewels of truth" that should be placed "in the framework of the gospel" (Ellen G. White, *Gospel Workers*, p. 289)?

   a. Heb. 9:11, 12 – Salvation through the blood of Christ, and Christ's mediation

   b. Isa. 14:12–14 – The "great controversy" theme and the character of God

   c. 1 Thess. 4:16–18 – The second coming of Christ and the state of the dead

   d. Dan. 8:14; Rev. 14:6, 7 – End-time prophecy, including the judgment-hour message

   e. John 14:15, 16; Rom. 6:23 – God's covenant of love, expressed in the Ten Commandments (law) but balanced by the mercy seat (grace) and the seventh day Sabbath

"In the holiest I saw an ark; on the top and sides of it was purest gold. On each end of the ark was a lovely cherub, with its wings spread out over it. Their faces were turned toward each other, and they looked downward. Between the angels was a golden censer. Above the ark, where the angels stood, was an exceeding bright glory, that appeared like a throne where God dwelt. Jesus stood by the ark, and as the saints' prayers came up to Him, the incense in the censer would smoke, and He would offer up their prayers with the smoke of the incense to His Father. In the ark was the golden pot of manna, Aaron's rod that budded, and the tables of stone which folded together like a book. Jesus opened them, and I saw the ten commandments written on them with the finger of God. On one table were four, and on the other six. The four on the first table shone brighter than the other six. But the fourth, the Sabbath commandment, shone above them all; for the Sabbath was set apart to be kept in honor of God's holy name. The holy Sabbath looked glorious—a halo of glory was all around it. I saw that the Sabbath commandment was not nailed to the cross. If it was, the other nine commandments were; and we are at liberty to break them all, as well as to break the fourth. I saw that God had not changed the Sabbath, for He never changes" (Ellen G. White, *Early Writings*, pp. 32, 33).

7. Given that there has been so much distortion throughout the centuries, is "church" really a necessity in the believer's life? Is God somehow in the church? (Matt. 16:16–19; 1 Peter 2:6–10; Heb. 12:22, 23)

   Yes! The church was established by Jesus Himself, and He chose twelve disciples as its first members, representing the twelve tribes of Israel and tying the Old and New Testaments together. The church is the new "Israel." The existence of false religious bodies should not discourage us from becoming part of God's church.

8. What indication do we have that tells us that Jesus loves the church? (Eph. 5:25–27; Rev. 1:12–20)

   He died for each person who makes up the body of Christ, and He watches over it yet today.

9. How was the organization of the early church set up, which serves as our pattern today? (Acts 6:1–7; 14:23; 15:1–3)

   As needs arose, church leaders (deacons and elders) were appointed to minister to others. If there was a theological issue, council meetings were called and delegates were appointed to address the issue and come to a biblical consensus.

10. How were members added to the church? (Acts 2:41–47)

    The church grew through baptism of new members.

11. There were only eight people saved on Noah's ark. What does Peter say is the antitype that now saves us? (1 Peter 3:18–22)

    According to Peter, the antitype is baptism. Today when someone is baptized they also join the church. Of course, it is not the church per se that saves us, but the message of that church.

Our early believers often used the term "ark of safety" to refer to the church. This, then, is the Bible's fifth ark! In Noah's day, the people who listened to him had a choice to either get on the boat or not. It is no different today. All four arks we identified in lesson one were and are "arks of safety." The following quote provides us insight into the ark of safety and our role in sharing this message with others.

"There is work to be done for our neighbors and for those with whom we associate. We have no liberty to cease our patient, prayerful labors for souls as long as any are out of the ark of safety. There is no release in this war. We are soldiers of Christ, and are under obligation to watch lest the enemy gain the advantage and secure to his service souls that we might win to Christ" (Ellen G. White, *Testimonies for the Church*, vol. 5, p. 279).

Bibliography

The Holy Bible, Douay/Confraternity Version. New York: P. J. Kenedy & Sons, 1961.

White, Ellen G. *The Acts of the Apostles*. Mountain View, CA: Pacific Press Publishing Association, 1911.

———. *Christ in His Sanctuary*. Nampa, ID: Pacific Press Publishing Association, 1969.

———. *The Desire of Ages*. Mountain View, CA: Pacific Press Publishing Association, 1898.

———. *Early Writings*. Washington, DC: Review and Herald Publishing Association, 1882.

———. *Gospel Workers*. Washington, DC: Review and Herald Publishing Association, 1915.

———. *The Great Controversy*. Mountain View, CA: Pacific Press Publishing Association, 1911.

———. *Manuscript Releases*. Vol. 8. Silver Spring, MD: Ellen G. White Estate, 1990.

———. *Patriarchs and Prophets*. Washington, DC: Review and Herald Publishing Association, 1890.

———. *Prophets and Kings*. Mountain View, CA: Pacific Press Publishing Association, 1917.

———. *Testimonies for the Church*. Vol. 5. Mountain View, CA: Pacific Press Publishing Association, 1889.

We invite you to view the complete
selection of titles we publish at:

www.TEACHServices.com

Scan with your mobile
device to go directly
to our website.

Please write or e-mail us your praises, reactions, or
thoughts about this or any other book we publish at:

TEACH Services, Inc.
P U B L I S H I N G
www.TEACHServices.com ● (800) 367-1844

P.O. Box 954
Ringgold, GA 30736

info@TEACHServices.com

TEACH Services, Inc., titles may be purchased in bulk for
educational, business, fund-raising, or sales promotional use.
For information, please e-mail:

BulkSales@TEACHServices.com

Finally, if you are interested in seeing
your own book in print, please contact us at

publishing@TEACHServices.com

We would be happy to review your manuscript for free.